Dmytro Shestakov

When Businesses Test Hypotheses

A Four-Step Approach to Risk Management for Innovative Startups

With a foreword by Anthony J. Tether

T0286137

UKRAINIAN VOICES

Collected by Andreas Umland

The book series "Ukrainian Voices" publishes English- and German-language monographs, edited volumes, document collections, and anthologies of articles authored and composed by Ukrainian politicians, intellectuals, activists, officials, researchers, and diplomats. The series' aim is to introduce Western and other audiences to Ukrainian explorations, deliberations and interpretations of historic and current, domestic, and international affairs. The purpose of these books is to make non-Ukrainian readers familiar with how some prominent Ukrainians approach, view and assess their country's development and position in the world. The series was founded, and the volumes are collected by Andreas Umland, Dr. phil. (FU Berlin), Ph. D. (Cambridge), Associate Professor of Politics at the Kyiv-Mohyla Academy and an Analyst in the Stockholm Centre for Eastern European Studies at the Swedish Institute of International Affairs.

Dmytro Shestakov

WHEN BUSINESSES TEST HYPOTHESES

A Four-Step Approach to Risk Management for
Innovative Startups

With a foreword by Anthony J. Tether

Bibliographic information published by the Deutsche Nationalbibliothek
Die Deutsche Nationalbibliothek lists this publication in the Deutsche
Nationalbibliografie; detailed bibliographic data are available in the Internet at
http://dnb.d-nb.de.

Bibliografische Information der Deutschen Nationalbibliothek
Die Deutsche Nationalbibliothek verzeichnet diese Publikation in der Deutschen Nationalbibliografie;
detaillierte bibliografische Daten sind im Internet über http://dnb.d-nb.de abrufbar.

ISBN-13: 978-3-8382-1883-0
© *ibidem*-Verlag, Stuttgart 2024

Printed in the United States of America

Contents

Foreword

This book bridges theory with actionable tenets of hypothesis testing. The author delves into the nuances of maintaining agile flexibility, reimagining capital deployment, and the art of timely pivots amidst unfolding startup uncertainties. The narrative, peppered with real-world startup sagas, ensures readers can vividly see the application of each principle.

Dmytro Shestakov's "When Businesses Test Hypotheses: A Four-Step Approach to Risk Management for Innovative Startups" is a compass for the startup brigade that will guide them through the modern entrepreneurial journey.

Dr Anthony J. Tether
Former Director of the U.S. Defence Advanced Research Project Agency (DARPA)

Annotated Table of Contents

The Strategic Flexibility of Startups

This chapter delves into understanding the management concepts of innovations, particularly in the context of businesses and startups. It gives a clear distinction between innovative projects, products, processes, affiliated uncertainties, and risks, ensuring that readers have a comprehensive understanding of each concept and a holistic picture of innovative startup risks. The challenges businesses face when evaluating innovative startup projects using traditional valuation methods, such as Discounted Cash Flow and Real Option Analysis, are discussed, along with the need for managerial flexibility to navigate these complexities. The chapter sets the stage for introducing the Hypothesis Testing Framework presented in Chapter II, offering a more practical and effective approach for managing and accessing the strategic flexibility of innovative business projects.

Innovation and Startup Management

The author clearly differentiates between innovations, regular products, and innovative products and projects, emphasizing the importance of understanding their unique features and management abilities in today's competitive business environment. Gaining a solid understanding of these differences is vital for successfully dealing with the challenges associated with innovative ventures. The author clarifies the methodological approach necessary for innovation project management, emphasizing its importance as a foundation for effectively overseeing the success of startups and other innovative projects. In doing so, the author provides a well-defined classification system for various aspects of project management, including project, innovation, innovative, technology, and innovation project management.

This taxonomy enables a thorough analysis of the differences between several traditional concepts, ultimately helping business professionals better understand and navigate the complexities of managing innovative ventures.

Evaluating Uncertainty and Risks

The author looks at the challenges of using traditional methods to evaluate innovative startups and examines the concepts of uncertainty and risk in depth, taking into account their various types and the associated opportunities that may arise in business situations. In the discussion of this book, the challenges of differentiating between general market uncertainty and specific uncertainties that businesses face in the real world are explored. The author also delves into the strategic approach of intentionally addressing and managing specific uncertainties by leveraging a company's unique, proprietary knowledge as a means to gain a competitive advantage. This comprehensive analysis highlights the crucial importance of understanding and effectively dealing with uncertainties in the realm of business, particularly when navigating the complex landscape of innovative products and startups.

Applied Logic of Real Options

The author demonstrates the logic behind real options by examining a straightforward business case, shedding light on how managerial flexibility operates in practice. Thus, by explaining the main types of options and their relevance to managing startups, the author also emphasizes the value of real options as a tool for entrepreneurs navigating the uncertainties associated with innovation. The in-depth exploration presented in this book equips entrepreneurs and startup product managers with the knowledge to make informed decisions and react nimbly to rapidly changing market conditions and manage the dynamic challenges of fostering and scaling innovative ventures.

Differentiating Innovations

The author delves into the various classifications of innovation, seeking to clarify and resolve inconsistencies by offering a well-rounded understanding that encompasses multiple aspects. This approach includes examining innovation in terms of types, levels, degrees, centricity, and dimensions such as modular and architectural, sustaining and incremental, disruptive, breakthrough and radical, demand-side and supply-side, as well as business-model and technology innovations.

The author also underscores the limitations of popular methods such as design thinking and the stage-gate model, implying that a more complex approach to understanding innovation is crucial for thriving in today's competitive business landscape. Thus, by addressing these distinctions and presenting a comprehensive taxonomy, the author aims to provide entrepreneurs with a valuable tool to better identify, navigate, and capitalize on different types of innovation. This clear and concise framework allows businesses to strategically position themselves in the market, tailor their approach to innovation management, and ultimately drive growth and success in an increasingly competitive landscape.

The Hypothesis Testing Method

This chapter presents the Hypothesis Testing Method in detail, explaining the four-step process that allows businesses to assess the potential success of innovative products while accounting for various development stages and inherent risks. The author underscores the critical role of evaluating the strategic flexibility of startups by introducing the hypothesis testing framework and demonstrates its applicability and relevance in various business scenarios. In addition, the chapter discusses the issues of mathematical accuracy and subjectivity that may arise when using the hypothesis testing method and advocates for adjusting risk evaluations using benchmark multipliers and internal rate of return (IRR) logic.

Assessing Strategic Options

The author analyses the pitfalls associated with customer-centricity, product commoditization, and differentiation challenges. This section discusses the assessment of strategic flexibility using well-known conventional methods such as Discounted Cash Flow (DCF), Decision Tree Analysis (DTA), and Real Options Analysis (ROA). This book section emphasizes the drawbacks of these techniques in accurately capturing the risks linked to innovative startups, explaining the shortcomings through the lens of deterministic cash-flow approaches, contingency logic, capital-at-risk perception, and both classic and risk-neutral probabilities. The author makes a strong case for the necessity of an alternative method that more effectively addresses the distinct challenges and uncertainties inherent in the innovation process.

The Hypothesis Testing Framework

The author emphasizes the necessity of moving from a limited product-centric mindset to a more comprehensive view that encompasses the entire project lifecycle and incorporates flexibility as a core aspect. This framework sheds light on and provides a comprehensive understanding of the nature of innovation in startups by introducing five principal hypotheses that can be further broken down into specific assumptions, which exhibit convexities and overlap as the project progresses, contingent upon the degree of innovativeness. A detailed comparison is provided between the Hypothesis Testing Method (HTM), Stage-Gate Model (SGM), and lean approach, highlighting their key distinctions in the context of proactive, agile, iterative, and incremental decision-making processes that are crucial for managing and evaluating innovative projects effectively.

Four-step Hypothesis Testing Method

The author outlines a four-step process for evaluating the appeal of an innovative product, factoring in its development and implementation stages, as well as the associated risks. This approach is demonstrated by examining an investment case involving a disruptive startup in its initial idea stage. By following this four-step process, entrepreneurs and managers can gain a better understanding of the potential success of their startups and make strategic decisions that maximize the chances of achieving their business objectives.

The author also tackles the concerns of mathematical accuracy and subjectivity in the multiplier approach used in the case study above within the context of high uncertainty of innovations. Two perspectives are explored to mitigate this subjectivity: Analyzing market depth using the TAM-SAM-SOM approach and determining the required rate of return adjusted for risk. The discussion acknowledges the challenges in finding benchmark revenue multipliers for startups and introduces the concept of Internal Rate of Return (IRR) to calculate risk-adjusted growth multipliers.

Startups and Economic Prosperity

In this chapter, the author investigates the role of innovation-driven economies in fostering postwar recovery and the significance of startups and venture capital industries in promoting economic growth. The Silicon Valley role model is discussed as a methodical and scaled example of successful economic development. The HTM is considered a potential catalyst for the systemic development of innovation ecosystems and startups, especially in countries facing postwar economic recovery. By connecting the book's central theme of strategic flexibility in innovative startups to real-world business scenarios, this chapter demonstrates the broader implications of applying the HTM, ultimately showcasing its value for businesses and startups alike.

The Secret Sauce of the Israeli Miracle

The essence of the Israeli miracle, as an innovation-driven economy and postwar recovery, is examined in the context of fundamental ecosystem development. The author highlights the crucial role of startup and VC industry predecessors and their innovative project focus, such as the United States Defense Advanced Research Projects Agency (DARPA), the Israeli Maf'at Agency, and the Office of the Chief Scientist. This analysis underscores the importance of fostering a strong innovation ecosystem and the significant impact that government-backed initiatives can have on driving economic growth and recovery in challenging circumstances.

Piloting Silicon Valley

The author delves into the establishment of the United States DARPA and the proliferation of the triple helix model as one of the most significant and transformative economic development frameworks of the 20th century. This model contributed to the emergence of Silicon Valley and facilitated the transition from closed, centralized innovations to an open-centric approach that promotes collaboration, idea networking, and coopetition. By fostering the development of a conducive infrastructure, the triple helix model has become instrumental in driving innovation and reshaping the business landscape, enabling organizations to thrive in increasingly competitive markets.

Postwar economic recovery

The author examines the economic progress of Ukraine prior to the large-scale Russian invasion in February 2022, focusing on the country's shift toward an innovation and knowledge-driven economy. This transformation was propelled by the exceptional growth of startup and IT ecosystems, which played a crucial role in transitioning from an oligarch-dominated system to an entrepreneurial one. Implementing the HTM is seen as a catalyst for the systematic development of innovation ecosystems and startups, particularly vital for postwar economic recovery. The author emphasizes the importance of further research on this topic to better understand its implications and potential benefits for future economic development.

Introduction

Solving problems and challenges no matter what they are, innovations bring value to people. Either brand new or slightly bigger than existed before, these values exist in the form of new products. In today's rapidly evolving business landscape, there are numerous approaches available for estimating the potential of innovative projects, including discounted cash flow, venture capital method, real options approach, comparison method, and replication cost, among others. Furthermore, a wide range of automated tools has been developed to facilitate the implementation of these techniques.

Despite the availability of such methods, investors often find it challenging to compare and assess these techniques in terms of their objectivity, accuracy, and capacity to handle the inherent uncertainties associated with innovative projects, products, or startups. This difficulty stems from the fact that the focus in evaluating innovative projects tends to be predominantly on the end result, typically monetization, rather than on the intricate process of creating value from the ground up while effectively managing uncertainties and risks along the way.

Existing methods for estimating innovative projects often overlook the importance of a comprehensive understanding of the entire innovation process, from idea conception to product development, and the various stages in between. This oversight can result in a limited perspective on the nature of the risks and uncertainties involved, which can ultimately hinder the accurate evaluation of an innovative project's potential value.

To overcome this challenge, it is crucial to develop and adopt a more holistic approach that goes beyond simply examining the end result. By placing a greater emphasis on the complex process of value creation and the management of risks and uncertainties, investors and entrepreneurs alike can gain a deeper understanding of the true potential of an innovative project, product, or startup, ultimately leading to more informed decision-making and, ultimately, greater success in the realm of innovation.

During the evaluation of a project's value, focusing solely on the outcomes of the later stages often results in the neglect of risks associated with earlier stages in the product lifecycle. Investors traditionally account for the uncertainty component by employing a discount rate, which aims to represent the aggregated risks of the entire project in a single figure. However, this approach still emphasizes the final results of the project, primarily in terms of expected cash flows, leaving investors unable to fully comprehend the true nature of the risks associated with innovative products. Consequently, their ability to manage these risks effectively is limited.

On the other hand, an innovative startup project, whether corporate or individual, can be viewed as a series of hypotheses requiring validation. Such projects can be broken down into various assumptions associated with specific stages, such as idea generation, prototyping, minimum viable product (MVP) development, basic version creation, and scaling. By testing these assumptions throughout the project's evolution, uncertainty can be reduced, and the degree of inherent risk can be better understood.

Therefore, a more comprehensive evaluation of a startup should account for all stages of its creation, considering the underlying assumptions and the nature of the associated risks. This approach enables a more accurate estimation of the project's value, taking into account the diverse options available at each stage. By adopting this perspective, investors and entrepreneurs can better manage risks and make more informed decisions, ultimately leading to more successful innovative ventures.

The aim of this book is to propose to look into innovation from a conceptual point of view, concentrating on the primary stages of their creation toward implementation and marketing and using an incremental delivery perspective. Shifting the focus from end results to the complex delivery process, we suggest a new approach to understanding innovation projects and their risks in a wider perspective than it is used to be considered.

The HTM considered in this book suggests a set of hypotheses that cover every innovative product aimed at commercialization and all aspects of their creation. We assume that in its fullest configuration, an innovation project always consists of the five high-level hypotheses that can be further decomposed into smaller assumptions. These are the following: team competency, technological capability, customer value, business model, and market depth. As the project progresses, these five hypotheses exhibit convexities and overlap, depending on the degree of product innovativeness, allowing for proactive risk management through validation from the very inception of a project.

By considering these five core hypotheses and their interactions, the HTM framework provides a comprehensive framework for understanding and managing the risks associated with innovation projects. This approach empowers entrepreneurs, investors, and other stakeholders to make informed decisions, ultimately leading to more successful and sustainable innovative ventures.

By breaking down each hypothesis, we gain a deeper understanding of a project's uncertainties and risks, as well as the array of investment and management options available. This in-depth analysis allows for a more comprehensive and accurate assessment of innovative startups. The HTM is highly practical and applicable to any project aiming for monetization, serving as a foundational concept for crafting innovations by clearly recognizing their risks and effectively evaluating their nuanced value.

In conclusion, the widespread adoption of the proposed method has the potential to serve as a powerful instrument for systemic economic development and the implementation of innovations. By embracing this approach, we can foster the growth of robust technological and innovation ecosystems, ultimately driving progress and prosperity in various sectors of the economy.

*"If you want something new,
you have to stop doing something old."*
Peter Drucker

I. The Strategic Flexibility of Startups

Innovation and Startup Management

Innovation is the lifeblood of differentiation in today's rapidly evolving landscape. It sparks economic growth and promotes development by introducing novel ideas, products, and processes that alter the way we think, consume, and create goods and services. It is hard to imagine the contemporary world without innovation, as they have become an integral part of our daily lives and continue to shape our future. Playing a crucial role in enhancing production processes, reducing costs, updating product offerings, and improving the quality of goods and services, innovation is essential for the successful implementation of effective management principles. It has emerged as a key driver of progress and a vital factor in securing competitive advantages in the modern era.

In a world characterized by relentless change, embracing innovation is not only a necessity for businesses and societies but also the cornerstone of human advancement. By fostering a culture of innovation, we can unlock new possibilities, drive sustainable growth, and propel our civilization toward a more prosperous and inclusive future.

Innovation is accelerating at an unprecedented pace in today's knowledge-driven and science-based economy, fueled by rapid advancements in technology, global connectivity, and shifting consumer demands. In such a dynamic environment, companies must continually adapt and evolve to maintain their competitive edge and ensure long-term success.

A thorough understanding of innovation and its nature is essential for grasping the nuances that differentiate traditional investment evaluation techniques from more flexible and adaptive approaches. At its core, innovation encompasses the process of developing and implementing novel ideas, products, technologies, or methodologies that address specific market gaps, solve existing problems, or cater to unmet societal needs. These outcomes are introduced into the market with commercial or practical objectives in mind, aiming to create unique value propositions that resonate with customers and differentiate businesses from their competitors.

Indeed, by adopting a contemporary perspective on innovation, we can emphasize its role as a systematic and structured approach to creating and cultivating unique value for customers. This entails examining each stage of the innovation process, from the inception of an idea and its development to prototyping, market testing, and eventual launch. Furthermore, it involves identifying and addressing potential risks and uncertainties associated with each stage, as well as considering the various factors that may impact innovation success, such as market trends, competitive forces, and technological advancements.

In this context, businesses and organizations must foster a culture that embraces innovation, encourages open-mindedness, and supports the exploration of unconventional ideas. This includes investing in research and development, adopting agile methodologies, and establishing strategic partnerships with other industry players, research institutions, and start-ups. Moreover, they should prioritize continuous learning and improvement, adapting their strategies and processes based on feedback, market insights, and evolving customer needs.

Thus, by integrating innovation into their core business strategies, companies can remain competitive, agile, and prepared for the challenges of the future. By proactively addressing potential risks and uncertainties, they can maximize the chances of successfully launching ground-breaking products and services that redefine markets and create lasting value for customers.

In recent years, projects have become an increasingly prominent organizational structure within companies that are involved in the development of new products, services, and processes. The systematic and well-managed development of innovations can only be achieved if there is a clear and consistent set of actions in the form of a project. A project, in this context, refers to a temporary effort that aims to create a unique product, service, or result by reorganizing human, financial, and material resources to complete a specific set of tasks. These tasks must meet predetermined quantity and quality goals while adhering to the constraints of time, resources, and external circumstances.

An ordinary project typically involves a high degree of predictability with respect to its expected outcomes and the necessary resources required for their realization (Fig. 1.1). This predictability stems from a clear understanding of customer needs, the desired product specifications, the development process and methodologies to be employed, the team members and stakeholders involved, and the business model for monetization.

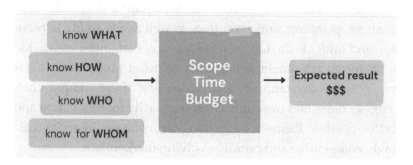

Fig. 1.1. The nature of an 'ordinary' project
Author: Dmytro Shestakov

An innovation project, on the other hand, serves as a tool for facilitating the transition from an idea or invention to an innovation, which is a product that is ready for use and scaling. Simultaneously, an innovation project also encompasses a set of defined and consistent processes that govern the implementation of this transition. Due to the inherent uncertainties and complexities associated with innovation, the outcomes of an innovation project may deviate from the initially planned objectives. This deviation is one of the key features and fundamental risks associated with venture investing and startup management.

Innovation projects differ from traditional ones in several significant ways. First, they often entail a higher level of uncertainty regarding the final product, the technological and methodological approaches, and the market reception. Second, innovation projects typically involve a greater degree of collaboration, requiring input from a diverse range of stakeholders, including customers, suppliers, industry partners, and academic institutions. Finally, innovation projects demand a more flexible and adaptive approach to management, which may necessitate the use of iterative, agile methodologies that allow for continual refinement and adjustment based on feedback, learning, and market insights.

As a result, innovation projects require a deeper level of analysis, planning, and execution, as well as the ability to manage and mitigate the inherent risks and uncertainties associated with the development and launch of novel products and services. By understanding and addressing these unique challenges, companies can enhance their capacity for innovation and better position themselves for long-term success in an increasingly competitive and rapidly evolving marketplace.

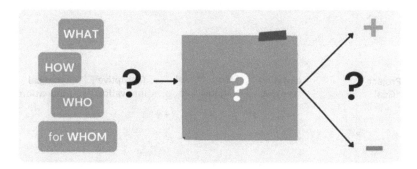

Fig. 1.2. The nature of an 'innovation' project

Author: Dmytro Shestakov

We consider a project innovative if the scope of work to achieve its goal or technology for its development, the predicted accuracy of the final results and their practical applicability (in terms of functionality or emotional perception by customers) cannot be determined with acceptable managerial accuracy proven by previous experience (Fig. 1.2).

By its nature, a project always involves the creation of a unique result, something new, and has certain risks. The main difference between projects is the degree of their innovativeness, i.e., The higher the level of innovativeness, the higher the level of uncertainty and risks of scattering future project results (Fig. 1.3).

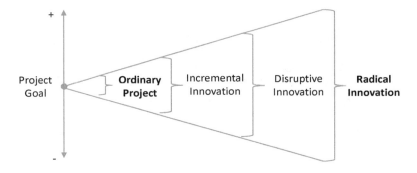

Fig. 1.3. Relation between the level of innovativeness and the uncertainty of a project

Author: Dmytro Shestakov

In comparing ordinary and innovation projects, it is essential to carefully examine the achievability of their goals, as well as the degree of uncertainty and the corresponding risks that accompany these endeavors. Ordinary projects, in contrast to their innovative counterparts, are characterized by a lower degree of uncertainty and risks of deviation from the expected results. This is because ordinary projects typically rely on established technologies and methodologies, which provide a solid foundation for project management and execution. The goals and outcomes are, therefore, more predictable and achievable.

In the case of innovative projects, a higher degree of innovativeness translates to increased levels of uncertainty and risks. This increase stems from the fact that innovative projects are built upon a greater number of untested hypotheses and assumptions. Consequently, project managers and stakeholders face significant challenges in defining the objectives, scope of work, and technologies utilized within these innovative projects. In other words, the less predictable nature of innovative projects stems from the need to experiment, explore, and discover new insights, making it more challenging to predict the precise outcomes and practical applicability of the project's final results.

The experimental nature of innovation projects means that innovations are often elusive, and their specific characteristics cannot be precisely determined until the hypotheses have been tested and previously inaccessible information has been uncovered. This inherent uncertainty creates substantial difficulties in assessing the investment attractiveness of an innovation project using conventional methods, which may not be well suited to account for the unique features and risks associated with such projects.

A prerequisite for the manageable success of a startup is following a methodological approach to innovation and project management. Innovation, as the creation and use of new knowledge, should be based not on chance but on systematic research and timely development in response to internal challenges of the company and external signals of the market. An important tool to do that is project management, which is an integral part of innovation management.

The definition of innovation management is often replaced by innovative and technology management. However, their nature differs. Innovative management relates to changes in what managers do and how that basically can create long-term benefits for the company. In turn, technology management is a process that includes the management of the development and implementation of particular technological capabilities to form and achieve the organization's strategic and operational goals. Technology management is how a company uses resources to create innovations over time and in the context of technological changes.

Meanwhile, innovation management is a framework consisting of many components, including continuous knowledge, product management, and commercialization if necessary. It is the provision of an adequate structure and environment for creativity. In turn, the Product Development and Management Association's Innovation Management Framework considers three key elements: competencies, dimensions and levels.

The framework identifies five organizational competencies that successful innovation teams possess: idea management, market management, portfolio management, platform and project management. A team must be proficient in all five competencies to reliably and repeatedly produce differentiated products and services. Competencies are not processes but the basic capabilities of innovation.

Second, the framework breaks down each competence into five dimensions: strategy, organization and culture, processes, techniques and tools, and metrics. The dimensions cross-cut each competence and represent the management activities needed to build robust and durable innovation management capabilities.

Successful late-stage startups and innovation companies look beyond their boundaries and pay attention to their environment. The last part of the framework addresses the unique innovation challenges and activities found at three levels of the environment: the firm, the industry, and the macro-environment.

Innovation project management is based on principles of innovation management and project management. At the same time, even though innovation and project management have been developing as independent disciplines, the most effective way to manage innovation is to use project logic. Projects are widely used to initiate critical changes in a company, not only to create and monetize new products. Additionally, as changes come as an outcome of successful project development, the skills and competencies related to change management and managerial flexibility are an integral part of innovation project management.

Exercise Questions

Reflect on the information provided about Innovation and Startup Management. Take some time to answer the following questions to practice your comprehensive understanding and their application in real-life scenarios.

1. What are the key differences between innovative products, services, and processes?
2. Consider real-world examples for each category.
3. What are the key differences between project and product management?
4. Think of ordinary and innovation projects. What are the key differences between them? Provide examples from your own experience for each category.
5. What is the relationship between the level of innovativeness, uncertainty, and risks? What kind of risks have you experienced? How did you measure and manage those risks?
6. What are the key differences between innovation management, innovative management, and technology management? Which of these have you applied in your professional experience?
7. Consider the PDMA's framework of innovation management. Which aspects of this framework have you applied in your professional work?
8. What distinguishes project management from innovation project management?

Evaluating Uncertainty and Risks

Evaluating uncertainty in innovative projects is unquestionably a multifaceted and intricate undertaking, given the extensive assortment of methodologies and approaches accessible to practitioners. These range from the time-tested Discounted Cash Flow (DCF) method to more sophisticated and advanced techniques such as Real Options Analysis (ROA). Each of these approaches comes with its own unique set of strengths and limitations, making it a herculean challenge to identify a universally applicable solution that can effectively evaluate the value and risks associated with various types of innovative projects.

The development, adaptation, and improvement of investment project evaluation methodologies throughout history have predominantly been driven by the need to overcome the shortcomings of conventional approaches that depend heavily on DCF. Before the 1960s, organizations relied primarily on two indicators of project attractiveness: the payback period and the accounting rate of return. Unfortunately, these simplistic metrics were insufficient, as they failed to take into account the time value of money and the varying levels of risk associated with different projects. With the introduction of the DCF method, a new chapter began in the realm of project evaluation, offering financial analysts and decision-makers a more powerful and efficient tool to assess project risks and investment attractiveness.

Approaches grounded in DCF, such as the widely recognized and commonly utilized Net Present Value (NPV), are generally known for their simplicity and ease of comprehension. These methods typically rest on projected cash flows throughout the entire duration of a project, with these flows being discounted at a rate that accurately reflects both the time value of money and the degree of risk intrinsic to the project. Within the context of DCF, investment decision-making follows a relatively simple logic: when comparing two mutually exclusive projects, the one with the higher NPV takes precedence. Consequently, an NPV greater than 0 indicates that a project is considered worthy of investment.

However, despite the popularity and apparent simplicity of DCF-based approaches, their suitability is limited to situations in which the future can be predicted with a considerable degree of certainty. For projects burdened with a high level of uncertainty, these methods fall short in providing accurate evaluations, as actual cash flows may deviate markedly from projections or may be altogether missing. To effectively manage risks and make informed decisions, investors should focus on assessing the range of potential actions in the future (managerial flexibility), depending on the course of events and the outcomes of experimentation and learning, rather than solely estimating a project's cost based on projected cash flows.

In light of the significant impact that innovation uncertainty has on project evaluation, the importance of time and managerial flexibility cannot be overstated. This flexibility includes a variety of options, such as the ability to postpone, abandon, expand, or terminate an investment project at a specific stage of its development. Since DCF-based methods possess limited capacity to effectively evaluate managerial flexibility and adapt to changing circumstances, ROA was developed as a more suitable alternative. It has gained widespread use in resource-intensive R&D projects within industries such as oil & gas and pharmaceuticals, among others.

It is the case that ROA has attracted considerable attention and interest in project management research literature since the 1980s. Created and implemented in response to the inadequacy of traditional DCF approaches in coping with the challenges posed by innovation and uncertainty, ROA draws upon the methods that form the foundation of the classic Black-Scholes-Merton financial options theory. This connection enables the evaluation of managerial flexibility and the consideration of project pivoting options during various stages of development.

Indeed, by implementing ROA in their evaluation processes, organizations can more effectively navigate the inherent uncertainties that accompany innovative projects, ensuring more informed decision-making and, ultimately, achieving improved project outcomes. Although DCF methods still hold relevance and value in the evaluation of more predictable and less uncertain projects, the integration of ROA has become an essential component for managing the complexities and uncertainties associated with highly innovative ventures. As such, organizations that aspire to succeed in today's rapidly changing and competitive business landscape must be prepared to embrace the latest evaluation methodologies and techniques to stay ahead of the curve and achieve long-term success.

We consider uncertainty and risk as different and interrelated concepts. Uncertainty is something unknown that we cannot solve in a deterministic way, so-called known unknowns, or something unknown that we can only get known and solve over time, unknown unknowns. In turn, a risk is the adverse effects associated with the onset of uncertainty.

Uncertainty and risks are inherent in any innovative project and startup, and the only difference is their degree and ratio. However, the level of uncertainty of a project should not be considered a purely negative phenomenon, as there is an opportunity on the one hand and a risk on the other, i.e., the possibility of increasing the profitability of the project or the risk of reducing it.

The specifics of innovation projects are that there can be many more potential opportunities than the risks of possible losses; that is, they combine both a high level of uncertainty and a high expected return. Opportunities and risks are interdependent concepts, so there is no reason to focus on reducing the risk without considering the associated opportunities, just as it is not recommended to use the opportunity without taking into account the relevant risk.

Extending the view from a narrow risk to broad uncertainty, you get a chance to assess relevant opportunities and analyze the project from the perspective of flexibility in decision-making. Uncertainty is directly related to innovations, as you never know exactly what processes, methodologies, technologies, or whatever should you use to create and monetize them.

Uncertainty can be divided into market, specific and private. Market uncertainty is associated with the price volatility of an asset caused by market price fluctuations. Market uncertainty is more or less predictable and is usually a function of external factors for a project as well as correlates with general economic trends. In other words, the source of market risk is an external environment that directly affects a project's cash flows. In fact, market risks are minimally dependent on managerial skills, decisions or processes when you develop new products. However, you can, to some extent, anticipate them and consider making investment decisions.

On the other hand, there is a high level of uncertainty about external non-price conditions, such as the destructive impact of new technologies, changing customer needs, the behavior of market incumbents, and the reduction of product lifecycles. It is called specific uncertainty, which is associated with internal factors and does not correlate with general movements in the economy. Accordingly, the specific uncertainty narrows to specific or diversified risk, which directly depends on the internal component of a project.

However, classification of project uncertainty strictly in the dichotomy between market and specific is a simplification of the real world, as there are cases when you cannot diversify them at all. This means that under various circumstances, you may not be able to trade a project on the market and thus provide market risk management by sharing it with other participants, or you may not be able to diversify the project-specific risks as well.

Moreover, investors and entrepreneurs may knowingly agree to some specific uncertainties, for example, when a project has more proprietary information or special knowledge on specific uncertainties than competitors. Thus, consciously retaining such uncertainties, they can expect a higher return. In this case, it is a private uncertainty, the main feature of which is that you can keep it intentionally and somehow manage it, even if you cannot diversify it.

In the context of the uncertainty of startups, traditional DCF-based valuation methods focus more on risks than on opportunities and available managerial options. For innovation projects, a DCF approach takes into account risks by applying a high discount rate but ignores much higher potential rewards. This bias leads to the abandonment of promising innovative projects, characterized by a high level of uncertainty and a wide range of flexibility.

Real options logic, on the other hand, recognizes and includes risks, opportunities and entrepreneurial options when evaluating innovations. This makes it possible to allow for flexibility of available decisions and to minimize investment risks. Real options provide an opportunity not only to assess the investment potential hidden behind the uncertainty of a startup but also to look at risks as a manageable matter throughout the project lifetime, depending on decisions made.

Therefore, you can rethink the capital at risk, conventionally perceived as the total amount of investment in the whole project, in the iterative logic of testing underlying hypotheses and uncertainty distributed throughout a project lifecycle depending on particular decisions. As a result, the nature of the uncertainty, which includes risks on the one hand and opportunities on the other, becomes clear and measurable.

An understanding and assessment of the available entrepreneurial flexibility of a startup become fundamental for its success. This means that such flexibility can relate to choosing a problem to solve, a technology stack to use, a configuration of a proposed solution, a price and business model, marketing channels, and so on. On the other hand, the team can design ideas, conduct a dialog with customers and verify the problem, create a prototype and minimum viable product (MVP), test it based on voice-of-the-customer (VoC), bring a product to market, etc.

Meanwhile, teams unable to manage uncertainties abandon the boldest, most forward-looking and promising ideas, preferring the more conservative ones. However, in the long run, in terms of a team's ability to respond to changes in a dynamic competitive environment, such a choice is doomed to decline.

Exercise Questions

Reflect on the information provided about Evaluating Uncertainty and Risks. Take some time to answer the following questions to practice your comprehensive understanding and their application in real-life scenarios.

1. How do uncertainty and risks differ, and how are they interrelated in the context of innovative projects?
2. Explain the concept of known unknowns and unknown unknowns in the context of uncertainty.
3. What are the differences between market, specific, and private uncertainties? Provide examples for each.
4. Discuss the limitations of the discounted cash flow (DCF) method when evaluating innovative projects with high uncertainty.
5. Explain the real options analysis (ROA) approach and its advantages over traditional DCF methods in dealing with uncertainty and risk in innovative projects.
6. How does managerial flexibility impact the evaluation of innovative projects? Give examples of different types of managerial options.
7. Describe the importance of understanding and assessing entrepreneurial flexibility in managing uncertainty and risk in startups.
8. Reflect on a real-life scenario where an innovative project or startup encountered uncertainty and risk. How did the organization manage these challenges, and what lessons can be learned from that experience?

Applied Logic of Real Options

Basically, an option provides the right to take specific actions, such as buying or selling an asset on predetermined terms or under certain conditions in the future. Since real options arose from financial options, the terminology for both types is common. Financial options relate to financial assets such as stocks and bonds and are commonly traded on stock exchanges. Real options relate to real assets, such as real estate, investment projects, and intellectual property.

Each option has an underlying asset, which is the basis and the subject of the option. For a real option, the underlying asset, for example, is the project itself. A real option is a right, not an obligation, to take certain actions on the underlying asset, which may include abandoning the project, extending it, signing a contract or postponing a decision for the future.

Suppose that StarJet[1] is a public company with shares traded on a stock exchange at $50 per share. On the one hand, investors expect an increase in the value of shares of the company through the development and implementation of innovative technology. On the other hand, a sharp drop in the company's share price is possible due to the uncertainty of market sentiment. That is, an investor can buy StarJet's shares at $50 per share or an option, the right to buy (call option) or to sell (put option) shares of the company (underlying asset) at a predetermined price at a predetermined time (European option) or at any time before a predetermined date (American option).

By purchasing a $5 call option, which gives the right to acquire StarJet's shares in one year for $50 without any obligation, an investor expects the price of the company's shares to increase by at least $5. If the market value of StarJet's shares increases by not more than $5, an investor has the right to refuse to buy the

---

1   Names of the mentioned companies are fictional.

shares. If the share price rises, let's say, by $12, an investor exercises their right under the option, buys the Company's shares for $50, and sells them at a market price of $62. As a result, an investor receives a profit of $7 after deducting the option-purchase expenditures.

By purchasing a $5 put option, which gives the right to sell StarJet's shares in one year for $50 without any obligation, an investor expects the price of the company's shares to decrease by at least $5. That is, if the market value of StarJet's shares falls to $30, an investor will sell the company's shares for $50 and receive a profit of $15 after deducting the option value. If the value of StarJet's shares falls no more than $5 from the sale price under the option, i.e., not less than $45, an investor has the right to refuse to sell shares.

The option logic allows an investor to take advantage of favorable opportunities and, at the same time, minimize the risks of significant losses if the initial assumptions are wrong. That is why real options became an important strategic tool for business management, as they are the basis of strategic planning and investing under conditions of uncertainty.

Similar to financial options, if the expected result is assessed as unfavorable, the real option is not to be exercised. Comparing financial and real options, an opportunity to invest in a project is similar to owning a financial call option. This means its underlying asset is the present value (PV) of cash flows of the investment project, while the exercise price represents the investments necessary for its implementation.

Providing the circumstances are favorable, and the PV of the expected cash flows of the project is greater than the PV of investment costs, the exercise of the option, i.e., investing in the project, is appropriate because the NPV of the project is positive in this case. However, in the event of an unfavorable course and refutation of major assumptions, the project can be terminated to minimize losses. In other words, an investor may consider the investment opportunity in terms of optimization of capital-at-risk, i.e., not as the total amount of required investments but as the minimum capital needed to exercise the option and test the respective underlying assumption. This is the gradual disclosure of a project's potential at each stage of its development.

A put option is the opposite of a real call option. Suppose that AISoft is a leader in the automation of production processes, the main activity of which is research and software engineering in the artificial intelligence domain. The company has recently invented an innovative algorithm and is interested in developing a new product by applying this technology. Since the potential market for the product is uncertain, AISoft wants to minimize the financial risks of investing in this project. Thus, the company considers the option to sell the technology if underlying assumptions are refuted. In turn, SuperCar company, which specializes in the production of electric vehicles, is interested in the technology of AISoft and in developing its software for autopilots.

AISoft and SuperCar sign a real put option agreement that entitles AISoft to sell their technology to SuperCar for $10 million at any time within two years. On the other hand, to get a chance to buy this technology, SuperCar buys an option and pays AISoft $1 million. After the first year of project implementation, AISoft refutes the customer value hypothesis and decides to exercise the put option by selling the technology to SuperCar for $10 million.

Real options can be compound or simple. A compound option is an option whose value depends on the value of another option but not on the value of the underlying asset (expected cash flows). Compound options are quite common in multiphase projects, where the launch of one stage depends on the successful completion of the previous stage, i.e., when one has a choice to continue developing a new product (move to the next stage), abandon further development (exit the project) or postpone it for a certain period of time.

The value of a simple option depends on the value of the underlying asset (expected cash flows). Simple options include a deferral option, option to expand, option to contract, option to abandon, option to choose, and switching option. A deferral option takes place when there is a choice to invest in a project or one of its stages today or postpone a decision until the uncertainty about the underlying assumptions is less and the prospects are more predictable. It is obvious that a deferral option exists for almost every investment project; however, using it can be unsafe due to the risk of earlier entry of competitors into the market, which shifts the attention of investors in favor of time-to-market.

An option to expand provides for the possibility of increasing investment in the project in the future and is a common practice among venture capitalists and angel investors. Instead, an option to contract provides the right to reduce the amount of investment, including by selling a part of assets, if market conditions are unfavorable for further development of a project.

An option to abandon provides an investor with the possibility to exit a project or close it. This option is especially valuable when the NPV of a project becomes insignificant, the probability of significant losses is high, and the investor has an opportunity to refuse further investment and participation in a project at an early stage.

An option to choose provides an investor with an opportunity to choose among the options available in a project, including the option to defer, expand, contract and abandon the project. An investor may not exercise the option, i.e., keep it open and continue working on the project or take advantage of any of other available options. The main advantage of this type of real option is the ability to choose, depending on which it can be considered both put (contract or abandon) and call (defer or expand) options.

A switching option provides for the possibility of transitioning a project to another mode of operation, alternative production process, technology, market, etc. The value of the switching option increases depending on the degree of innovativeness of the project, i.e., the number and level of uncertainty of the hypotheses and assumptions underlying it. A switching option can also be both call and put.

Exercise Questions

Reflect on the information provided about the Applied Logic of Real Options. Take some time to answer the following questions to practice your comprehensive understanding and their application in real-life scenarios.

1. How do real options help in dealing with uncertainty and risks in innovative projects? Can you recall a situation from your experience where using real options could have improved decision-making under uncertainty?

2. Explain the difference between call and put real options, and provide examples of situations where each might be used in the context of innovative projects. Have you encountered a situation where you had to decide between exercising a call or put option in a project?

3. Describe the various types of simple real options (deferral, expand, contract, abandon, choose, and switching options). Can you share examples from your own experience where one or more of these options were utilized in dealing with uncertainties in a project? How did these options impact the project's outcome?

4. What are compound real options, and how are they different from simple real options? Give an example from your professional experience where a compound real option was used in a multiphase project. What challenges did you face, and how were they resolved?

5. Reflect on the role of real options in strategic planning and investing under conditions of uncertainty. Can you think of an example where the use of real options helped a company navigate through uncertain times and make better decisions?

6. Discuss the potential drawbacks and limitations of using real options in managing uncertainty and risk in innovative projects. Have you encountered a situation where real-life option did not provide expected benefits or created additional complications? How was it handled?

7. In your professional experience, have you ever utilized real options as a decision-making tool for managing uncertainty and risk? If so, please describe the project, the options considered, and the results. If not, how do you think applying real options could improve your decision-making process in future projects?

8. How does the concept of real options complement traditional financial analysis tools such as net present value (NPV) and discounted cash flow (DCF)? Can you share an example where combining real options with these traditional methods improved the evaluation and decision-making in an innovative project?

Differentiating Innovations

Innovation activity results in an innovative product in the classic sense or service, method of production (technology), or another socially useful result (social innovation). An essential characteristic of an innovative product is its practical application, but not necessarily commercialization. Depending on the application of innovation, external or internal, there are product innovations and process innovations. Product innovation involves the introduction of an improved or new solution to a problem to enter the market and meet users' needs. Process innovation relates to the introduction of improved or new elements in the production or other business processes of an organization.

In turn, innovation as a process consists of various phases and stages from the beginning of creation (initiation and planning) to the implementation and introduction of an innovative product. Initiation is about analyzing the context, identifying the existing problems, and designing and evaluating alternative solutions, while implementation solves these problems through product development.

Analyzing innovation as a process through the prism of its evolution, i.e., In the direction of customer orientation, cyclicity, and open interaction, it is safe to say that the process of creating innovation consists of five basic stages, namely, understanding and analyzing the problem, generating ideas, finding a solution, and developing and introducing results. Of course, these stages may vary in common sense, but fundamentally, they will not differ in any other commonly used methodology or practice.

Thus, within the design thinking approach, one of the most common in innovation development, there are five stages: empathizing, defining, ideation, prototyping and testing. First, you gain an empathic understanding of the problem you are trying to solve. A substantial amount of information is gathered to use during the next stage, defining the problem and developing the best possible understanding of customers, their needs, and problems underlying the development of a product. Second, you analyze observations and synthesize them in order to define the core problems to be solved. Third, you generate solution ideas to a problem to further prototype and test a product.

Another widely used approach is the stage-gate model. It generally focuses on the innovation process and consists of six stages: discovery, including idea generation, scoping, building a business case, development, testing and validation, and finally, launch.

In the process logic of innovation, the stages should be distinguished between continuous and time-framed activity, which is project logic. Understanding and analyzing a problem, generating ideas and finding the best solutions is a continuous process of product management. On the other hand, product development and implementation relate to the time-framed project logic.

Therefore, we can say that an innovation process consists of a process and project as a means of transition from an idea or invention to the actual innovation, that is, a product ready for use and scaling. In turn, an innovation project is a set of defined and sequential, cyclic or parallel processes to implement the transition from an idea to a product.

The typology of innovations, along with their definition, understanding of goals and necessity, is a very common and controversial topic. Existing taxonomies are either fairly abstract or rather narrow and do not provide a more or less complete idea and understanding of the subject. In general, innovations are distinguished by level, degree and dimension.

By level, they can be modular and architectural. Modular innovations relate to changes at the level of individual components. In contrast, architectural innovations, which are how components link together, involve a change in the nature of the interaction between the main components of a product or process.

By degree, innovations are mostly distinguished as sustaining or incremental, disruptive, and breakthrough or radical. According to Christensen, sustaining innovations targets established high-margin customers, or so-called high-end customers, in existing markets with better performance than previously available. However, Christensen's view about sustaining innovations is narrowed to a customer-oriented perspective, whereas it can also be considered from the internal use of an organization. In a broader view, sustaining innovation corresponds to the common term incremental innovations, which means updating, increasing productivity, or modifying existing products, services, or methods within existing market, technologies or organizational processes.

The widely spread paradigm of disruptive innovations introduced by Christensen indicates that the market competition trajectory is disrupted and redefined by introducing products and services that are not as good as currently available. Instead, they are simpler, more convenient, and less expensive. There are also low-end disruptions for less-demanding low-margin existing customers and new-market disruptions that enable a whole new population of people to begin owning and using them.

On the other hand, terming Christensen's approach the demand side, Gans considers supply-side disruptions that are particularly difficult for incumbents to adopt and offer competitively because they involve changes in the entire architecture of a product rather than in the components themselves. Therefore, it is not so much that firms choose not to respond to disruptive innovations but that there are some sorts of them that they cannot respond to.

Instead, breakthrough or radical innovations are mostly understood as significant or completely new and unique technological changes that lead to a new vision or paradigm shift in general and can be either disruptive or not.

By dimension, we separate business-model and technology innovations. Business-model innovations are comprised of changes in (i) value proposition, (ii) value chain, which is how the product is produced, marketed, distributed, delivered and serviced, including a firm's suppliers, retailers, distributors, and partners, or changes in (iii) the target audience, e.g., switching to non-consumers or narrowing customer segments. In turn, technology innovations can relate direct changes in a product, changes in technological and production processes, and changes in supporting technologies (indirect production and operating technologies).

Exercise Questions

Reflect on the information provided about innovations. Take some time to answer the following questions to practice your comprehensive understanding and their application in real-life scenarios.

1. What is the key difference between product innovation and process innovation? Can you think of a situation in your experience where a company introduced a product innovation or a process innovation, and what was the outcome?

2. Describe the five stages of the design thinking approach and explain how they can be used in the innovation process. Have you ever been a part of a team that utilized the design thinking approach? What were the challenges and successes during the process?

3. Briefly explain the stage-gate model and its relation to the innovation process. Can you recall a project where the Stage-Gate Model was implemented? How did it affect the project's progress and outcome?

4. What are the two main types of innovations by level, and how do they differ? In your experience, have you observed any examples of modular or architectural innovations? How did these innovations impact the organization or industry?

5. Explain the difference between sustaining or incremental, disruptive, and breakthrough or radical innovations by degree. Can you think of a time when you witnessed or participated in the development of one of these types of innovations? What were the key challenges faced during the process?

6. What are the three main components of business model innovation, and how do they contribute to the overall innovation process? Have you experienced them within an organization you were a part of? How did it change the way the organization operated?

7. Provide an example of a technology innovation that has influenced the market and explain how it has changed the industry. Have you ever been directly affected by a technology innovation in your field? How did it impact your work and the industry as a whole?

8. Can you think of a real-life scenario where an organization successfully implemented a combination of product and process innovation? Describe the case and its impact on the organization's success. Have you ever been involved in a project that combined product and process innovation? What were the key takeaways from that experience?

9. How does understanding the various types and dimensions of innovation help organizations in their strategic decision-making processes? In your professional experience, how has understanding different types of innovation aided in making better decisions for the organization?

10. In your opinion, which type of innovation is most crucial for organizations in today's competitive market environment? Explain your reasoning. Based on your experience, which type of innovation has had the most significant impact on your industry, and why?

"Strategy is not the consequence of planning, but the opposite: its starting point."
Henry Mintzberg

II. The Hypothesis Testing Method

Assessing Strategic Options

In the increasingly dynamic environment of modern times, maintaining competitiveness by adapting to constant changes has become even more challenging. As the focus on customer-centricity continues to grow, businesses often find their vision of the future narrowing, pushing them into the trap of competition and engaging in a constant race to improve the quality of existing products and services. Furthermore, when such improvements are accompanied by price competition, it leads to the commoditization of the product, meaning a decrease in its added value and identity (differentiation) simultaneously. Conversely, when improvements occur without price competition and businesses strive to maintain their margins, it triggers the emergence of disruptive innovations, putting the existence of the business as a whole at risk.

In such circumstances, a proactive strategy or a game of anticipation becomes not just an advantage but a prerequisite for a company's viability, even though uncertainties can be difficult to predict. To adapt quickly to abrupt and unpredictable changes, which can only be managed at the time of their occurrence, a company must possess flexibility. Achieving this flexibility requires a strategy that reduces periods of instability through rapid and effective change and is impossible without the systematic identification and evaluation of external factors.

The flexibility of a strategy can be considered from different angles. First, from the perspective of strategy as a plan, the capabilities and competitive advantage of a company take the central role. In this case, companies need to leverage their internal strengths, mitigate internal shortcomings, and neutralize external threats to adapt to dynamic external conditions in a timely and effective manner. Second, considering strategy as a pattern that combines a company's goals, procedures, and actions in a unified whole can be replicated and somehow predicted. In this case, flexibility becomes an element of the strategy itself by respective policies and procedures. Strategy as a practice, on the other hand, shifts focus to the practical competence of a manager as a strategist. The goals and practices of implementing the strategy are dependent on the social system of a company, meaning how employees interact with each other.

Flexibility refers to the ability to respond to unpredictable changes and swiftly and timely adapt to new environmental conditions by changing the course of action and transforming oneself. Flexibility is the extent to which a variety of capabilities are available and the speed at which they can be activated. Flexibility can be created through new strategic initiatives not only by developing new products but also by deformalizing processes, leading to process innovation, and by fostering interaction within teams, which accelerates decision-making and enhances the ability to tackle new challenges.

Strategic forecasts burdened with high-level uncertainty create a paradox for a strategy as such in terms of relying on it in the present. One way to overcome this paradox is to consider strategic flexibility as a set of possible precautionary actions against known unknowns and possible reactive actions in the event of unknown unknowns. It is evident that implementing preventive actions as part of a proactive response strategy significantly activates innovation activities.

On the other hand, strategic flexibility can also be viewed as strategic maneuverability, referring to a variety of potential strategies and the degree to which a company can rapidly transition from one strategy to another. This perspective allows businesses to adapt and pivot as needed in the face of ever-changing market conditions and challenges.

Each management decision can be measured with some reliability in monetary terms because it has a value, that is, it involves the cost of its implementation and, ultimately, directly or indirectly affects the expected cash flows of a company. In other words, each individual decision can be evaluated and compared using the approaches of evaluation of investment projects. Accordingly, strategic flexibility as a set of management options can be assessed.

As we already know, the greater the level of innovativeness is, the greater the uncertainty. This means innovation by nature has greater variability of possible scenarios, and greater flexibility is needed to react reactively to unknown unknowns. That is, strategic flexibility comes to the fore in terms of evaluating an innovative project not only as an approach to a more accurate assessment of its investment attractiveness but also as an approach to finer risk management.

In a broad sense, a project is attractive for investment if its value, the difference between project revenues and costs of its implementation, aka project value, is positive. As part of traditional approaches, namely, Discounted Cash Flow (DCF) and Decision Tree Analysis (DTA), the quality of project valuation is related to how effectively they take into account underlying factors such as cash flow, discount rate, and managerial options to pivot the project for DTA.

The cash flows of an investment project consist of costs and revenues during its projected life cycle, namely, capital expenditures and net income at the implementation stage and costs and returns in the case of individual managerial decisions. Accordingly, the essence of assessing the investment attractiveness of a project or individual managerial decision is to assess these two cash flows and bring them to present value using an appropriate discount rate. In other words, you use a discount rate to bring the future value of a project cash flow into its present value to factor in the risks of an investment project and the uncertainties of the future. Thus, the higher the risks, the higher the discount rate.

In turn, managerial options such as pivoting or killing the project, embedded practically into every project, present significant strategic value and thus must be considered when assessing the attractiveness of investment opportunities and the feasibility of certain managerial decisions. In other words, you should allow for strategic flexibility when analyzing the attractiveness and feasibility of startups and innovations; otherwise, you can reject projects with significant strategic value simply because of their inability to compete with ordinary ones whose evaluation models ignore the strategic potential and apply simplified risk assessment converted solely into a discount rate.

Traditional tools for evaluating investment projects and managerial decisions, such as DCF and DTA, rely on using the concept of the present or discounted value of a future cash flow (present value, PV). This means that money tomorrow is cheaper than money today, which is quite logical given the uncertainty associated with time:

$$PV = \frac{FV}{(1+r)^n}$$

In this relationship, PV is the present value of a future cash flow, FV is the future value or expected cash flow, r is the discount rate, and n is the number of time periods.

The DCF method exists in many variations, but they all mean the calculation of the net present value (NPV) of a project. In turn, the calculation of NPV also exists in several variations, which ultimately boil down to the difference between the net cash flow (NCF) of a project and investments in its implementation. Since NCFs are generated over a long period of project implementation (more than one year), they must be discounted, allowing for relevant risks and using a discount rate, as follows:

$$NPV = \sum_{t=0}^{n} \frac{NCF_t}{(1+r)^t} - \sum_{t=0}^{n} \frac{I_t}{(1+r)^t}$$

In this expression, *NCF* - net cash flow, *I* - investments, *r* - discount rate, *t* - time period, and *n* - number of time periods.

One of the main peculiarities of DCF is the application of a predominantly fixed discount rate for all cash flows during a project life cycle. On the other hand, you can also apply a relatively flexible discount rate, which is usually adjusted downward as the project progresses, which aligns with the logic of reducing risks over time.

In general, if the NPV of a project is greater than zero, we consider it an investment attractive. That is, if the sum of the expected NCFs discounted to present value is greater than the sum of the discounted investment costs, we treat the project as worthy of investment. Although the DCF method has gained popularity due to its versatility and simplicity, it has a number of significant shortcomings that limit its ability to allow for dynamism and variability in the modern world.

First, DCF's deterministic approach to estimating project cash flows is quite massive and clumsy to analyze the attractiveness and risks of a project in dynamics. Although this problem is partially solved by software solutions such as SAP and Oracle ERP systems or individual simulators such as Monte Carlo, it is resource-intensive both in terms of time and professional competencies required for such modeling. On the other hand, DCF provides a linear and fixed trajectory of achieving results that ignore the embedded strategic flexibility of a project. This distorts the assessment of attractiveness, especially for projects with a high level of uncertainty and projects that involve testing a wide range of assumptions. After all, the potential results of contingent managerial decisions, which can significantly mitigate the negative consequences, are not considered.

Second, the bottleneck of the DCF approach is its discount rate used for risk accounting, which consists of a risk-free rate and a risk premium for each individual project. In other words, the higher the level of uncertainty and risk of the project, the higher the level of risk premium you should use. That is, the discount rate accounts only for the negative side of uncertainty while ignoring the associated opportunities, which are greater than the potential losses, the greater the degree of innovativeness of the project. At first glance, this problem does not look significant, but if you evaluate a project with potentially exponential growth, say to the level of a unicorn, it is likely that you will use a moderate forecast of cash flows and discount them with a high risk-premium rate. On the other hand, the convergence of risks into a single discount rate makes it impossible to understand their nature and therefore assess them, which intuitively makes innovative projects less attractive than traditional ones.

Third, in the DCF logic, the investment required to implement a project is perceived as completely capital-at-risk. However, in terms of embedded managerial options, you can minimize capital-at-risk as the project evolves and key assumptions are confirmed or refuted. Ignoring this, you significantly distort the riskiness of innovative projects, resulting in the rejection of potentially attractive strategic opportunities.

Decision tree analysis (DTA), in contrast to DCF, is a much more effective method of evaluating innovative projects. Decision trees are also called decision diagrams and show a strategic roadmap visualizing alternative outcomes depending on available scenarios, the cost of making decisions, and the probabilities of such outcomes with financial consequences.

DTA is performed using a graphical representation of events in the form of branches in possible scenarios to determine the appropriateness of managerial decisions. In addition, DTA allows you to evaluate available options in terms of the project lifecycle and look at capital-at-risk from the contingency logic, that is, if-then logic, at each node of decision-making, such as go or no-go decision. DTA provides an understanding of the scatter of future results, that is, the maximum negative and positive values depending on the implementation of available strategic options at each stage of the project. This, in turn, gives an option to assess and therefore understand not only the potential threats but also the opportunities that, in the case of DCF, are rolled into the discount rate.

Basically, DTA is not an alternative to DCF but its extension for calculating the attractiveness of the project by discounting expected cash flows to present value using the appropriate discount rate. That is, in the decision tree analysis, you evaluate attractiveness as the sum of expected NPV for each of the possible scenarios weighted by the respective probabilities of their occurrence, which is called expected NPV (ENPV). The weak point in DTA is the probabilities used to weigh the obtained values, as they are subjective and, simultaneously, one of the most influential variables on the ENPV indicator. This causes fair contradictions when making decisions in favor of certain projects.

As we already know, due to the inherent uncertainty and inherent risks of innovations, consideration of underlying flexibility while evaluating innovative ideas and startups plays an important role in their design, development and implementation. However, traditional tools such as DCF and DTA do not reflect modern dynamics and turbulence caused by relentless changes in technologies, customer preferences, and disruptive solutions whatever and, thus, are hardly applicable to this task. Meanwhile, real options analysis (ROA) combined with DTA is a good solution.

Real options analysis gives the best ever-existing solution for mitigating subjective probabilities while using decision trees. Meanwhile, calculating the risk-neutral probability factor that underlies ROA-based project attractiveness ratios requires you to have a high level of acknowledgment in financial modeling and isn't easy and thus a very spread methodology for use.

Moreover, while real options analysis and DTA can consider a project at different time intervals, they do not cover the nature of the risks of innovations by default. Estimating startups and innovations, we propose a new perspective that allows you to overcome these obstacles and look differently at startup risk management.

Exercise Questions

Reflect on the information provided about Assessing Strategic Options. Take some time to answer the following questions to practice your comprehensive understanding and their application in real-life scenarios.

1. How does strategic flexibility help businesses adapt to changing market conditions? Can you recall a time when your organization successfully adapted to change by employing strategic flexibility?

2. Discuss the different perspectives from which flexibility of a strategy can be considered. Which perspective do you think is most relevant for your organization, and why?

3. What are the limitations of the discounted cash flow (DCF) method in assessing investment projects and managerial decisions, especially in the context of innovative projects? Have you encountered any issues with DCF in your experience? How did you overcome them?

4. How does decision tree analysis (DTA) differ from and extend the DCF method in evaluating innovative projects? What are the weak points of DTA?

5. Have you used DTA in your work? What challenges did you face, and how did you address them?

6. We briefly explain the role of real options analysis (ROA) in assessing strategic options and why it might be challenging to apply in practice.

7. Can you think of an example where strategic flexibility has played a crucial role in a company's success or failure? Explain the situation and how strategic flexibility influenced the outcome.

8. In your opinion, what industries or types of businesses could benefit the most from adopting a strategic flexibility approach, and why?

9. How would you recommend that a company improve its strategic flexibility to better adapt to the rapidly changing market environment?

The Hypothesis Testing Framework

In addition to the mentioned drawbacks of the traditional approaches to evaluating innovations, they narrow the logic to the finished product. It means you focus on assessing product-based cash flows, ignoring the whole product lifecycle. However, being the top of the iceberg, product sales miss contingent decisions, embedded flexibility, related uncertainties and risks underlying earlier product development stages.

An uncertainty mirrored by hypotheses that stipulate a project value. By calculating product-based cash flows, you obtain the NPV necessary to make appropriate decisions. However, based on the successful implementation of the project as a whole, a product-narrowed perspective disables understanding assumptions underlying its lifecycle. These are ideation, prototyping, finding product-market-fit, testing business-model, and only after you enter the market where product sales come. Therefore, to determine and evaluate the inherent risks of a startup, it is necessary to separate their types relevant to each stage of product development.

The stage-gate model (SGM) is the closest existing methodology to covering the uncertainties and risks of product development. It is based on the belief that product innovation begins with ideas and ends once it is successfully launched into the market. SGM includes four primary stages. The first two are scoping and design, and although they anticipate some early customer feedback, they do not account for team, technology and customer value uncertainties.

In turn, the third stage of SGM, development, also converges its sub stages from prototyping to creating a fully functional product into a one-view perspective. Thus, it disables you from determining inherent development risks in a more precise manner. Launch and scaling are final stages under SGM, meaning full-scale production, marketing and sales. After completion of each stage, the gate follows, where you need to decide whether to start the next stage or abandon the project (go or kill decision).

However, there is no doubt that the risks of not confirming the hypotheses persisting to later stages must be analyzed as early as possible. Needless to say, it can significantly minimize potential losses. Undoubtedly, SGM adds much more flexibility to project management than rigid waterfall logic. This is due to adding cyclicality at different stages and timely go-back logic. However, it is about project management rather than innovation risk evaluation.

On the other hand, the opposite skewness that gives the Lean approach is the focus on quick prototyping of a customer-oriented product rather than its launch, product-market-fit and scaling. This means that it does not account for the risks of later stages that SGM does. This is the principal distinguishing characteristic between the Hypothesis Testing Method proposed in this book and the Lean philosophy.

One more critical aspect considered approaches and methodologies ignore, especially from an investor perspective, is their inability to rethink capital at risk of innovation investment. Thus, it significantly affects the project's attractiveness.

Meanwhile, instead of SGM and Lean approaches, we consider proactive agile iterative and incremental logic to analyze and account for product risks at each stage of its development. Thus, innovation uncertainties are easy to understand and manage from the beginning of a startup. Such an approach enables you not only to consider go-or-kill decisions through the product lifecycle but also to include other options such as a pivot or postponement. Instead of quantifying the depth of the market and building detailed financial cash flow models, we emphasize shifting the focus to qualitative analysis of key assumptions at each project stage, that is, idea, prototype, MVP, market entry and scaling, and analyze how you can test them as early as possible.

We assume that in its fullest configuration, a startup always consists of the five high-level hypotheses that you can further decompose into smaller assumptions. These are the team competency, technological capability, customer value, business model, and market depth hypotheses, which have convexities and overlap during project progress depending on the degree of innovativeness and thus enable managing risks proactively by testing them from the very beginning of startup creation.

Understanding the decomposition of each hypothesis reveals a more detailed picture of the project's uncertainties and risks and the variety of available investment and managerial options. It enables a more comprehensive and accurate evaluation of innovation. The hypothesis testing method is practically applicable to any project, which makes it a conceptual basis for the creation and development of innovation by perceiving their risks in a much clearer manner and enabling assessment of their subtle value.

Before we go into the hypothesis testing method as a methodology to estimate the risks and attractiveness of a startup, let us consider the framework that gives fundamental clarity and understanding of the nature of innovation.

Hypothesis 1: Team Competence (H1)

The project team forms the basis for all activities, directly participates in major processes, and performs tasks for creating, developing and implementing a marketable product. The technical team should be able to create a prototype, MVP and a basic version of an innovative product. The business team should be able to draw the product concept, manage its development, develop a business model and implement sales strategy, and scale the product regarding both customers and nonusers.

The team competence hypothesis is present at every stage of a startup, starting with the idea until the scaling of the product created. This means that the team's competence generates end-to-end risks throughout the project's lifecycle. Due to the different specialization of technical and business teams and diverse activities throughout the implementation of innovation, the risk impact of the project is different depending on its stage.

At the prototype, MVP, and basic version stages, the technical team competence hypothesis (H1.2) has a greater impact than the business team competence hypothesis (H1.1) since the main tasks at these stages are creating the prototype, MVP, and basic version, respectively, and require substantial technical expertise. The business team begins to dominate after the business model (H4) testing during an MVP stage (see fig. 2.1), while the technical team continues focusing mainly on supporting and refining the product.

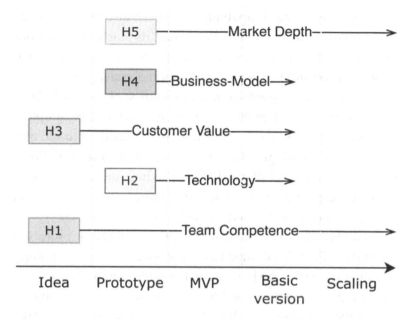

Fig. 2.1. Hypotheses of a startup in terms of product evolution
Author: Dmytro Shestakov

Hypothesis 2: Technological Capability (H2)

Innovation is created in a certain time period, where appropriate technological solutions and theories dominate and are available for use. Technology maturity can significantly affect the results of a startup and product implementation. The technological capability required to create and manage technical changes includes skills, knowledge and experience that often, but not always, differ significantly from those required to operate existing technical systems. The technology development capability allows you to choose and use technology with strategic purposes, create new methods, processes and techniques, and mostly offer new products.

The technological capability hypothesis also involves an assessment of the technology's complexity, its practical applicability, and the development level of supporting technologies that, in one way or another, affect the use of the underlying technology. An innovative product may also consist of several technological solutions, which implies multilayered levels of complexity, practical applicability, and the development of basic and supporting technologies. In fact, diversification of risks of different technological solutions does not reduce the whole uncertainty of the innovation project but rather creates multilevel risks that must be identified and managed by testing H2.

Incremental development of a product through prototyping and MVP, with a limited basic functional set, means creating an initial version of the innovation to enable potential customers to evaluate core features and to prove or deny its value, that is, testing the customer value hypothesis (H3), which lets you make a respective pivot or exit a project and thus stops losses at a minimum level. MVP allows you to focus more on knowing who your customers are, their habits, and how to attract and retain them. Therefore, the technological risk is being reduced as you progress through the development stages, which means that at the prototype stage, the risk is the highest, and at the market entry and scaling, it is the lowest.

It is evident that technologies used to create a prototype, MVP and basic version can be complex, and their practical applicability and level of development can affect the technological capability to accomplish necessary tasks and achieve the project goals.

Hypothesis 3: Customer Value (H3)

An innovation project always aims to meet existing customers' or users' needs or create a new, previously unknown demand.

While the marketing component reflected in the degree of customer commitment to the product is one of the basic concepts of innovation success, a startup producing an innovative product is eventually aimed at meeting customer needs. Therefore, the essence of the customer value hypothesis is to confirm the value of the product and the willingness of targeted users to use it.

A new product is valuable if it offers a better way to solve a problem. However, even if the product has some functional, emotional or social benefits, compared to other alternatives, a customer also takes into account the cost, time and efforts needed to use the product before acquiring it. That is, value is not just the quality and quantity characteristics of a product against those available on the market; it is the willingness of a customer to buy this product within the offered price model, which is reasonable to be tested before market entry and as a part of the business model hypothesis (H4) testing.

Hypothesis 4: Business Model (H4)

Technology or a product by itself has no single objective value. Their economic value remains latent until you commercialize them in some way by implementing a business model. The essence of a business model is in defining how you deliver value to customers, entice customers to pay for value, and convert those payments to profit. Following the project logic, the purpose of making a business model is to confirm the willingness of customers to buy a product for the offered price model based on a particular value chain and using designed marketing channels. Despite being competitive, an innovative product may still not find its customers through a poorly designed business model.

The business model of a startup should give clear answers to the following questions: how you create the product (supply chain), how you sell and deliver it, how you support and maintain it, how you attract customers, and how you benefit (mone-tization model). Without a proper business model, a technolog-ically innovative product will hardly penetrate the market, not to say create a new one, and disruptive innovation will not dis-rupt it.

Hypothesis 5: Market Depth (H5)

Investors always look at startups in terms of their commercial scalability. Innovations that satisfy a narrow customer category generally do not have significant demand among venture capi-talists.

The uncertainty about market depth relates not only to un-predictable volumes of possible revenues but also to the sources of revenue. Except you or not, you test the market depth hypoth-esis with regard to all, namely, (i) configuration of innovation (type, degree, dimension), the creation of which is envisaged by an innovation project, since different combinations of product characteristics may imply significant differences in the breadth and depth of a target market; (ii) value of the product you de-velop and the ability to meet the specific needs of customers; and (iii) scalability and access to new markets.

The hypothesis testing framework makes it possible to look at the project through the prism of the evolution of risks inherent in each stage of its development. If you breakdown the project for each of the hypotheses into basic assumptions, then you will receive a specific list for testing and, accordingly, working with risks at earlier stages of project implementation.

At the product idea stage, the team demonstrates mainly business competencies, developing product vision. As the pro-ject progresses, blind spots of the team appear, which you can reactively fill by attracting missing competencies and proac-tively strengthening the team through acceleration and other training programs. The customer value of a product can and should begin to be tested at the idea stage. To do this, use retrospective quantitative analysis — statistics, search queries, etc., as well as interviewing potential customers regarding the problem hypothesis, its relevance, existing direct and workaround solutions, and the actual intended solution of the team. To test the customer value of the product at the idea stage, marketers traditionally use focus groups and surveys. However, for startup products, these techniques do not work for a number of reasons.

The format of the focus group involves immersing respondents in the context, that is, immediately conditioning them to a specific vector of reflection. Second, the desire to be consistent in a social group forces respondents to adhere to a previously voiced position, especially if it coincides with the point of view of other participants. Third, the focus group format does not imply a deep discovery of the respondent.

Surveys at the idea stage do not work well because they exclude the possibility of open dialog, customer empathy, and the discovery of new hypotheses. The mess in, the mess out, so in order to get high-quality survey results, a more accurate formulation of product assumptions is necessary, which is almost impossible without interviews and empathy at the beginning. If surveys are good tools in the following stages of product development, focus groups are not.

In contrast, peer-to-peer interviews are a time-consuming customer discovery method but are the most profound. It allows you to test the initial assumptions from the triad of customer value, that is, problem-relevance-solution, discover new ones and form more accurate hypotheses for further testing at the prototyping and MVP stage.

The prototyping stage of the product opens up a number of opportunities to work with risks for all five hypotheses. The prototype goes through three main stages: graphic product design, dynamic prototype and proof-of-concept. The business team demonstrates competencies in creating a product design and dynamic prototype, testing the customer value hypothesis, developing and testing the business model, and market depth. The technical team develops a design, a dynamic prototype, and most importantly, a proof-of-concept or technological viability of the project. With the help of graphic product design, you can test the triad of the customer value hypothesis in a broader audience. First, face-to-face interviews, observations, and surveys were conducted. Second, peer-to-peer A/B testing is conducted before developing a dynamic prototype.

Experienced entrepreneurs start testing the business model hypothesis, in particular the willingness of a customer to pay for the product, even at the stage of the idea or graphic design. They ask the question during interviews or user surveys directly whether you are willing to pay or how much you are willing to pay. However, this is a huge mistake. The problem is that the psychological principle of consistency plays here again. That is, if the respondent has already said that he likes your product and is ready to use it, with a greater degree of probability, he will answer that he is ready to pay for your decision. However, such a response would be biased and unrepresentative.

Product design solves the problem of testing the hypothesis of the customer's willingness to pay for the product, which is the central hypothesis of the business model, if you use it in the form of a landing page where you drive the traffic of the target audience. A potential customer has the opportunity to choose the buy option, but since the product does not yet exist, he goes to the page with gratitude and an explanation that the release is planned for later. This is so-called smoke testing. Using this approach, you need to remember that it can cause a user disappointment from the path gone without a result, so it is also important to offer the user a reward, for example, a discount on a future purchase or, say, another perk.

In addition to testing the willingness to pay for the product, smoke testing with the help of the landing page enables testing the target audience and customer acquisition channels. When product development is technologically expensive, at the product design stage, it is advisable to start testing the market depth through the same smoke testing, flooding more target traffic compared to testing the business model.

The dynamic prototype is a continuation of testing the customer value hypothesis, the business model, and market depth. Its distinctive feature is that it allows you to collect user activity and behavior analytics about individual features and components of the product. This will enable you to move on to the development of a product MVP with a more accurate configuration and fewer associated risks.

MVP (minimum viable product) is the main stage of testing the hypothesis of the technological feasibility of a product. In terms of customer value and business model testing, a distinction is made between alpha and beta MVP. An alpha version differs from a beta MVP in that you test a product on a limited target audience to receive feedback and readiness to use it. Beta MVP enables you to test a product on a broad audience and validate the willingness of users to pay for it. The peculiarity of beta MVP is that users know it is a buggy product and are more tolerant of possible product failures. Obviously, beta MVP makes it possible for you to test other business model hypotheses, such as channels for attracting the target audience and the market depth hypothesis.

The basic version, from the point of view of product technology, is the core of the technology risk check. Depending on the complexity of the technology and the architecture of a core product, the basic version may differ significantly from the MVP. Otherwise, the difference between them, in terms of technological risks, will be insignificant and consists of bringing the product to market, that is, product launch. The same goes for the customer value hypothesis. Regarding a business model, at the basic version stage, you can confirm the willingness to pay for a product, the effectiveness of promotion channels and communication with the target audience by reaching the project's break-even point as a whole.

The scaling stage. In fact, here, you confirm or refute the market depth hypothesis. It is noteworthy that the classical approach to evaluating investment projects focuses on confirming exactly this hypothesis. Thus, the risks associated with the stages from idea to scaling are aggregated to the discount rate or, better to say, ignored. Figure 2.2 shows how classic NPV relies on projected cash flows, which you can achieve only if you successfully test the four hypotheses in the previous stages.

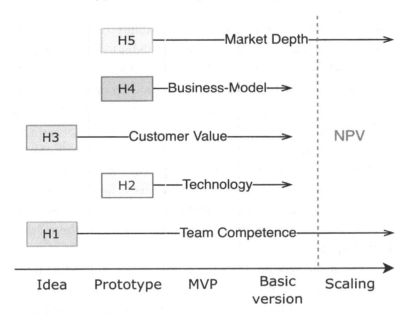

Fig. 2.2. Classic NPV vs startup development stages

Author: Dmytro Shestakov

Clearly, the hypothesis testing framework offers a broader and clearer perspective in understanding the uncertainty of startups. Moreover, it opens up the possibility for further assessment and management of associated risks, which we will discuss in the next chapter.

Exercise Questions

Reflect on the information provided about the Hypothesis Testing Framework. Take some time to answer the following questions to practice your comprehensive understanding and their application in real-life scenarios.

1. Have you ever encountered uncertainties and risks during product development in your organization? How did you handle them?

2. Describe how the stage-gate model (SGM) differs from the lean approach in regard to addressing uncertainties and risks in product development. Have you used either of these methodologies? What was your experience with them?

3. Explain the significance of the five hypotheses in the Hypothesis Testing Framework. In your experience, which of these hypotheses has been the most critical for a project's success, and why?

4. Think of any examples in which applying the Hypothesis Testing Framework could have helped in better understanding and managing a project's risks and uncertainties.

5. Explain how customer value can be tested at the idea stage of a product. What are the limitations of focus groups and surveys in this context, and why are peer-to-peer interviews more effective?

6. Describe the prototyping stage of a product and how it helps in testing and managing risks. What are the three main stages within the prototyping stage, and how do they contribute to overall risk management?

7. How does product design help in testing the business model hypothesis? What is "Smoke testing" and why is it an effective method for testing this hypothesis?

8. What is the difference between alpha and beta MVP, and how do they contribute to testing various hypotheses in the product development process?
9. How does the basic version of a product help in managing technological risks and other aspects of customer value and business model hypotheses?
10. What is the importance of the scaling stage in the Hypothesis Testing Framework, and how does it relate to the market depth hypothesis?

Four-step Hypothesis Testing Method

As we have already said, the higher the degree of innovativeness of the product, the greater the uncertainty in the final result, and the more cumbersome and incapable is the assessment of the attractiveness of a startup by classical approaches. Moreover, in evaluating a project based on its cash flows using NPV, there is a bulge in understanding the failure risks of a startup, as NPV relies heavily on the product scaling stage. Therefore, the hypothesis testing method allows us to shift the focus to the risk assessment of a project rather than keeping on sticking to rigid financial and market forecasts. Let us consider the simplified approach to assess the attractiveness of innovative product development, taking into account its implementation stages and inherent risks.

Let's say you're considering investing in an ambitious startup in the idea stage. You like the idea of the product, and you believe in the team. The product is at the cutting-edge of technology and looks very promising to become a future unicorn. The amount of investment required is $400k for development and market entry without taking into account the need for further rounds of attraction and equity dilution.

Step 1. Consider the possible scenarios for the development of the project and the decision tree through the prism of the hypothesis testing framework (fig. 3.1).

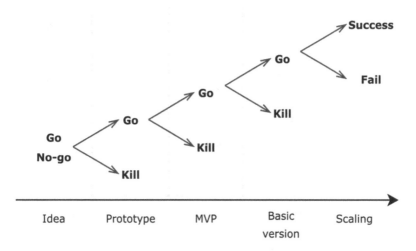

Fig. 3.1. Project decision tree through development stages

Author: Dmytro Shestakov

It is evident that at each stage of the project, there are at least two possible scenarios — confirmation of related hypotheses or their refutation. Accordingly, in the first case, you will continue the implementation of the project; in the second case, stop it. Thus, the kill or no-go decision option allows you to manage the risks of investment loss, that is, to minimize the capital under risk, depending on the results of hypothesis testing.

Let us say that at the idea, prototype, MVP, basic version and scaling stages, you need to invest $25k, $75k, $100k and $200k, respectively. Consequently, the capital at risk at the stage of making a decision to invest in the project is not $400k but $25k. Obviously, as the project progresses, the risks are reduced. It is intuitive. That is, the capital at risk, for example, at the second stage — prototyping, should be less than $100k because the uncertainty associated with testing hypotheses at the idea stage has become less (fig. 3.2.1).

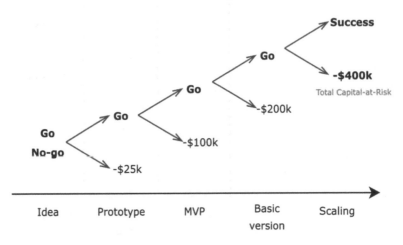

Fig. 3.2.1. Project decision tree and capital-at-risk

Author: Dmytro Shestakov

Step 2. We know how much you need to invest in the project at the decision-making stage. Therefore, the first extreme value of the expected result of the project in the form of the maximum possible loss is 100% of the invested capital in the startup (fig. 3.2.2).

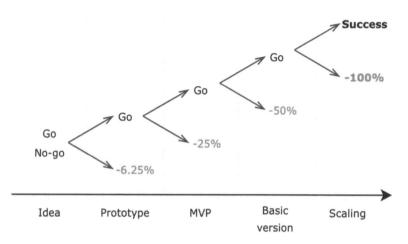

Fig. 3.2.2. Project decision tree and capital-at-risk

Author: Dmytro Shestakov

Step 3. The second extreme value of the expected result of the project is its future cost. Within the framework of traditional approaches, this is where the snag comes from since everything depends on cash flows, market volume, etc. However, the venture capital market works differently.

The fact is that the speed of the startup world is incomparably faster than all other industries. It is the most ruthless, and decisions are made as quickly as products die. Therefore, there is a so-called venture investor approach, or as we call it, the multiplier method. This means you use a certain multiplier of investments or possible annual revenue to estimate the possible future value of the project. Let us say it is 40 to the total investments required or $16 M of the project valuation at the scaling stage (fig. 3.3).

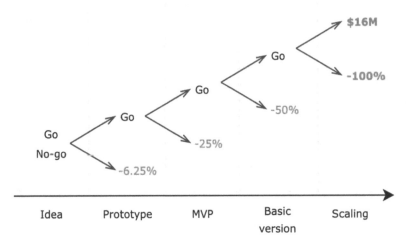

Fig. 3.3. Extreme values of possible outcomes of the project
Author: Dmytro Shestakov

Of course, this is a very subjective approach. That is the only way it seems at first glance. In our case, we evaluate the pre-seed stage of the startup. In practice, this means that if its lifecycle before the scaling stage takes more than two years and its capitalization is less than $5 M, this is an unsuccessful investment as, with such valuation, it'll be almost impossible to raise enough money for it further development not saying expansion.

Why is that? First, when a startup goes public, and this is an integral part of testing at least a beta MVP, there is a risk of its improved copycat by other startup entrepreneurs. Therefore, the delay in go-to-market is equal to the death of the product, at best clinical, when you finally started, but you were behind the faster guys. It means you will need more time and resources to scale. In other words, you have around two years to prototype, develop an MVP and bring to the market the basic version of the product.

Next, entering the market with MVP and some $50k for initial marketing may be enough, then marketing a basic version at the early scaling stage there is not. Another distinctive peculiarity of a startup is that with the successful validation of the product and business model, for further growth, you need first to invest capital in its promotion. That is, even though you have created a product that is in demand, without attracting additional investments in its scaling, you can forget about further development. Many startup entrepreneurs fail only because they do not know it and find themselves in a situation where they start fundraising too late, and the resources for it have already been exhausted.

In practice, you attract initial capital for scaling at seed and late-seed stages in the range of $1-5 M for 10-20% of equity, depending on the geography. Accordingly, the startup valuation range at this stage can be between $5-50 million, depending, among other things, on the project stage, the geography of the target market and the project headquarters. That is, the multiplier to the invested capital can range between 12-120. This is the average temperature for the ward without taking into account the potential for the exponential growth of a startup.

Remember that investor relations in a startup are an ongoing process. Who is your first customer? Most assume it is a user. No, this is an investor who believes in your product long before the user has the opportunity to hold it in their hands. The world of startups is a world of investors who look much more strategically than ordinary users. The latter, in principle, think limitedly, just for today, do not understand trends and do not even know half of the already existing better and more convenient products for solving their problems.

Step 4. To understand the current value of a startup, you need to move from right to left of a decision tree. That is, from extreme future values to the current state, called the backward

induction method. In our case, we know that the extreme negative value at the scaling stage is $400 K, and the extreme positive
value at the multiplier 40 is $16 M (fig. 3.4).

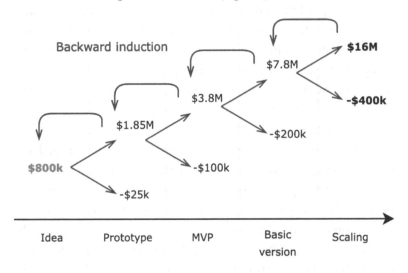

Fig. 3.4. Startup valuation on each development stage
Author: Dmytro Shestakov

To obtain the value of the project at the stage of entering
the market, you need to calculate the weighted average value of
the extreme indicators: -$400k and $16 M. Thus, the value at this
stage is $7.8 Moving from right to left, you similarly calculate
the values for each stage and come to the project value in the
amount of $800k at the beginning of its implementation.

Obviously, you may argue against using the weighted average approach here, as it returns us to the same issue of subjective probability discussed above. In addition, we would agree
and suggest that you should start using here more sophisticated
real options analysis (ROA), which you can read for free on my
LinkedIn profile https://www.linkedin.com/in/dmytro-shes
takov/.

From the point of view of mathematical accuracy of minimal error, the multiplier approach may seem like a kind of manipulation and does not spark trust due to its strict subjectivity. However, in the case of innovation, when the range of possible values depends on the wide range and degree of uncertainty of the underlying hypotheses, it is difficult to talk about accuracy in principle.

You can revise the subjectivity of the multiplier method for estimating possible extreme values from two angles. On the one hand, you can reach the multiplier through an express assessment of the achievable depth of the market and, therefore, the ceiling of possible returns, or, on the other hand, through the required rate of investment return adjusted for risk.

The most common method of express analysis of market depth is TAM-SAM-SOM. First, you consider the total market for your product, which is the total addressable market (TAM). Then, you narrow the TAM to the serviceable available market (SAM), which is a portion of the market you can acquire based on your business model, that is your target. Finally, you narrow the SAM to the serviceable obtainable market (SOM), a percentage of the SAM you can realistically capture.

In fact, the SOM is the ceiling of your possible revenue in principle, part of which you can achieve in the analyzed period. For example, if your SOM is $1B, you can accelerate revenue from zero to $25 M in three years. Thus, by multiplying such revenue by the industry benchmark multiplier, for instance, 2.0, you get a maximum exponential capitalization of the project in the amount of $50 M. Dividing the received cap by the amount of required investment yields a multiplier of exponential growth without allowing for risks.

However, finding benchmark revenue multipliers for startups is another challenge, which is more difficult than for mature businesses with publicly traded peers. The most operative way is to watch exits on close verticals and industries on the analytical service Crunchbase.com.

Consider the second alternative option for prompt estimation of the exponential growth multiplier using the required risk-adjusted return on investment. In portfolio investing, there is a concept of the internal rate of return (IRR) of the portfolio for a period. For venture investors, the IRR is 30-40%. This means that, on average, the portfolio should bring an annual return of 30-40% (at a compound interest), accounting for unsuccessful projects. If, say, the probability of startup success at an early stage is 10%, then the minimum expected risk-adjusted growth multiplier for three years will be in the range of 22-27 for the investments made without dilution.

Exercise Questions

Reflect on the information provided. Take some time to answer the following questions to practice your comprehensive understanding and their application in real-life scenarios.

1. Why is it essential to consider the kill or no-go decision option in managing the risks of investment loss in a startup project?
2. Explain the concept of the multiplier method and how it can be used to estimate the future value of a project.
3. Why is the backward induction method used to understand the current value of a startup, and how does it work?
4. What are the two alternative ways to revise the subjectivity of the multiplier method for estimating possible extreme values?
5. What is the TAM-SAM-SOM method, and how can it be used to assess the market depth for a startup project?
6. How can you use industry benchmark revenue multipliers or required risk-adjusted return on investment to determine the exponential growth multiplier for a startup project?
7. Think of the limitations and potential challenges of using the Hypothesis Testing Method in assessing the attractiveness of a startup project. How can these limitations be mitigated?

III.   Startups and Economic Prosperity

The Secret Sauce of the Israeli Miracle

After becoming independent in 1948 and continuously suffering from external hostilities caused by the 26-year war, Israel has settled as an innovation superstate that coins new technologies and has contributed to global economic prosperity for many decades. Sixty years ago, it exported mainly fruits, whereas now innovations generate 11% of its GDP and stand behind more than half of export volume, amounting to $70 billion a year.

The term "Israeli miracle" refers to the remarkable economic and technological growth that has taken place in Israel since its establishment as a nation in 1948. Despite being a small country with limited natural resources and facing significant security challenges, Israel has managed to build a thriving economy that is widely regarded as one of the most innovative and dynamic in the world.

The Israeli miracle is characterized by a number of key factors, including a focus on technological development and innovation, a culture of entrepreneurship and risk-taking, and a strong partnership between government, academia, and industry. Israel's government has played a key role in promoting economic growth by investing heavily in research and development activities, supporting the establishment of high-tech companies, and creating a regulatory environment that is conducive to innovation and entrepreneurship.

In recent decades, Israel's economy has been driven by its high-tech sector, which is focused on areas such as cybersecurity, biotechnology, and artificial intelligence. Israeli companies in these fields have become global leaders, with many of them achieving significant international success and recognition.

Despite the many challenges that Israel has faced over the years, including wars, conflicts, and political instability, the country has managed to build a vibrant and resilient economy that has become a model for others around the world. The Israeli miracle is a testament to the power of innovation, entrepreneurship, and perseverance, and it continues to inspire people around the world to pursue their own dreams of economic and technological success.

The quintessence of the Israeli miracle was comprehensive governmental assistance to the innovation and startup industry at the beginning before the VC layer appeared. It was implemented mainly through direct subsidizing research and development and entrepreneurship initiatives conducted by academics and businesses. For that, the Office of the Chief Scientist was formed in 1968 on the model and under the aegis of the American DARPA (Defense Advanced Research Projects Agency).

Switching from the linear innovation management model to the cooperative approach, later called the triple helix model, which was duplicated in Israel after its successful implementation in the US, has become the key trend in innovation development all over the world initiated by DARPA in the 1960s. Such transformation significantly changed the role, forms and methods of science, education, government and business cooperation in the innovation development lifecycle.

Under the triple helix model, universities take a strategic role in continuous innovation development at a national scale, and academics discover opportunities further to monetize their intellectual efforts in terms of loyalty and spinning out into startups. Investing in early-staged R&D-intensive initiatives carried out by universities, a government decreases respective risks that normally businesses would avoid taking on and invests in innovative and entrepreneurial culture among talented students and academics.

Therefore, close cooperation between business and academia ensures risks of further application and monetization of new developments. What is more, a separate layer of business appears—startups, who are fast, flexible, innovative and very well motivated, and with whom conventional big business cannot compete in terms of velocity but making corporate VC investments into multiples of newly grown solutions to face stiff competition.

The Israeli venture ecosystem has its roots in the country's focus on technological development, which began in the early years of its existence as a nation. Israel's government recognized the importance of investing in technology and innovation as a means of promoting economic growth and strengthening national security. In the decades since Israel's founding, the country has built a thriving ecosystem for entrepreneurship and innovation, particularly in the field of high technology.

The development of Israel's venture ecosystem can be traced back to the establishment of the Office of the Chief Scientist (OCS) in 1978, which was tasked with promoting and funding research and development activities in the Israeli private sector. The OCS played a key role in the growth of Israel's high-tech industry, providing grants and other forms of financial support to Israeli startups and helping to create a culture of innovation and entrepreneurship.

In the 1990s, Israel's venture ecosystem began to expand rapidly, with the emergence of a number of venture capital firms and angel investors who were willing to provide funding and support to early-stage startups. This growth was driven in part by the success of Israeli companies such as Check Point Software, which became one of the world's leading cybersecurity firms in the late 1990s.

Today, Israel's venture ecosystem is one of the most vibrant and dynamic in the world. The country is home to thousands of startups, as well as hundreds of venture capital firms and other investors who are actively seeking to support and fund new companies. The ecosystem is particularly strong in areas such as cybersecurity, artificial intelligence, and biotechnology, where Israeli companies are leading the way in developing cutting-edge technologies.

Israel's venture ecosystem has also become increasingly international in recent years, with Israeli startups and venture capital firms expanding their activities to markets around the world. Many multinational corporations have established research and development centers in Israel, attracted by the country's deep talent pool and its reputation as a global center for innovation and entrepreneurship.

A prerequisite of developing the innovation and tech ecosystem was the creation of the Israeli Maf'at agency (also known as MAFAT), the DARPA-like organization called "The administration for the Development of Weapons and Technological Infrastructure". It is an agency within the Israeli Ministry of Defense that is responsible for the research and development of new military technologies, as well as the testing and evaluation of existing ones.

The agency was established in 1969, following Israel's experience during the 1967 Six-Day War, in which the Israeli military had to rely on imported weapons and technologies due to a lack of domestic production capabilities. The Israeli government realized the importance of developing its own military technologies and set up Maf'at to address this need. Maf'at's primary mission is to develop cutting-edge military technologies that provide the Israeli Defense Forces (IDF) with a technological edge over its adversaries. The agency is also responsible for developing civilian technologies that can be used for military purposes.

Over the years, Maf'at has been involved in the development of a range of military technologies, including unmanned aerial vehicles (UAVs), missile defense systems, advanced intelligence systems, and more. The agency has also collaborated with various Israeli and international companies and research institutions to develop new technologies and bring them to market. Today, Maf'at continues to play a crucial role in the development of Israel's defense capabilities, and it is widely recognized as one of the most innovative and advanced military research agencies in the world.

As a continuation of Maf'at's efforts, the Office of the Chief Scientist (OCS) was established in 1978, with the goal of promoting and supporting research and development (R&D) activities in the Israeli private sector. OCS is an agency within the Israeli Ministry of Economy that is responsible for promoting and funding research and development (R&D) activities in the Israeli private sector. It provides grants and other forms of financial assistance to Israeli companies that are engaged in R&D, with the goal of supporting innovation and strengthening the Israeli economy.

The creation of the OCS was driven by Israel's desire to promote innovation and technological development as a means of strengthening the country's economy. In the years following its establishment, the agency played a crucial role in the growth of Israel's high-tech industry, which has become one of the most advanced and innovative in the world.

Under the leadership of the OCS, Israel has become a hub for cutting-edge R&D activities, particularly in the fields of biotechnology, information technology, and other high-tech industries. The agency has supported the development of a range of groundbreaking technologies, including the USB flash drive, the PillCam capsule endoscopy system, and the Iron Dome missile defense system.

Today, the OCS continues to play a critical role in promoting R&D activities in the Israeli private sector, with a focus on supporting innovation, entrepreneurship, and collaboration between industry, academia, and government. The agency provides funding and other forms of support to thousands of Israeli companies and research institutions each year, helping to drive innovation and economic growth in Israel and around the world.

While Maf'at and the OCS are both agencies within the Israeli government that are involved in R&D activities, they operate in different spheres. Maf'at is primarily focused on the development of military technologies, while the OCS is focused on promoting R&D activities in the Israeli private sector, including in fields such as biotechnology, information technology, and other civilian industries.

However, there is some overlap between the activities of Maf'at and the OCS. For example, Maf'at has collaborated with Israeli companies and research institutions in the development of civilian technologies that have military applications, such as cybersecurity and unmanned aerial vehicles. Additionally, the OCS has provided funding and other support to Israeli companies that are involved in the development of technologies with potential military applications.

In some cases, Maf'at and the OCS may work together to support R&D activities in areas that are relevant to both military and civilian applications. However, their primary areas of focus and responsibility are distinct, and they operate independently of each other within their respective spheres.

Piloting Silicon Valley

The turning point in the spread of the triple helix model was the formation of the U.S. DARPA. Affiliated with the Pentagon and formed after the Soviet Union successfully launched the first artificial satellite in 1957, DARPA was committed to the prevention of unexpected and undefeatable defense system military technologies run by other countries in the USA.

DARPA has been instrumental in propelling the U.S. to the forefront of technological innovation. Its model has had profound implications for economic and innovation development not only within the United States but also in other countries that have sought to replicate its success, including Israel. DARPA's influence is also evident in the Israeli venture ecosystem, which is characterized by high-risk tolerance, quick decision-making, and a focus on revolutionary rather than evolutionary innovation.

In addition to its direct projects, DARPA has also spawned other influential entities. Two such subsidiaries, for instance, are the Electronics Evolution Incorporated (EEI) and the Information Science and Technology Advisory Group (ISAT). EEI was a DARPA-funded project aimed at advancing electronics technology. It contributed to the development of integrated circuits, which laid the foundation for the modern electronics industry. The impact of EEI can be seen in everything from smartphones and computers to advanced military systems. ISAT, on the other hand, advises DARPA on future directions in computing and information science and contributes to the strategic planning of its projects. It has played a significant role in promoting advancements in areas such as artificial intelligence, cybernetics, and quantum computing.

Through its work and the work of its subsidiaries, DARPA has had an enormous impact on economic and innovation development. Its model of high-risk, high-reward innovation has propelled the development of numerous technologies that underpin modern society, including the internet, GPS, and many others. By promoting a culture of innovation and risk-taking, DARPA has helped create an environment in which technological breakthroughs are not only possible but also expected.

Therefore, what did DARPA implement so new and different? They changed the perspective from closed centralized innovations to an open-centric approach spreading collaboration, idea networking and coopetition by creating and nurturing relevant infrastructure. Determining top priority challenges and long-term national defense targets, they selected further development and implementation partners among academia and business. They then ensured project financing and supported orchestrating all that through their program managers. In addition, by seeing the significant impact of delegating strategic tasks to universities and startups on strategic competitive advantages, private businesses began following DARPA's approach and delivering their problems to the market, which provided increasingly more space for creativity for young engineers and entrepreneurs.

DARPA has directly supported the development and implementation of many breakthrough innovations, such as weather satellites, unmanned vehicles and robotics, stealth technology, etc. Their developments underlie a wide array of products presently used in every modern household, including integrated circuits and semiconductors, the Internet, cloud technologies, GPS systems, etc.

However, one of the most important and omitted things they did was the phenomenal implementation of what we now know as the Triple Helix model based on Stanford University, the intellectual heart of future Silicon Valley, together with San Jose State University, Santa Clara University and California University in Santa Cruz. In fact, DARPA's Silicon Valley project was a prototype of what Harvard's Professor Michael Porter later called a cluster-based economic development model in which the triple helix is an integral component for innovations.

Needless to say, what Silicon Valley has brought to the world of innovations and entrepreneurship. Apart from nurturing entrepreneurial mentality among talented youths and narrow-minded academics and building a modern shape of venture ecosystem, they have made a shift in perception of innovation risks toward their conscious taking and management paving the way for the spread of standards for new product development and hypothesis testing mindset.

The profound impact of DARPA's work is reflected not only in its direct initiatives but also in the wider ripple effects on industries, ecosystems, and the economy. For instance, DARPA's open-centric approach to innovation has altered the dynamics of traditional industry boundaries. This model has encouraged a wave of cross-industry collaboration and innovation, fostering an environment where industries converge and new sectors are born. It has also prompted a fundamental shift in how businesses, academia, and governments view and manage innovation. By showcasing the power of open innovation and the importance of risk-taking in the pursuit of breakthroughs, DARPA has helped to cultivate a cultural shift toward embracing uncertainty and failure as integral parts of the innovation process. This has resulted in a more dynamic and resilient innovation ecosystem that is better equipped to navigate the uncertainties of the future.

Moreover, DARPA's model has influenced the strategic thinking of organizations and governments around the world. Recognizing the importance of long-term strategic planning in driving innovation, many have adopted DARPA-like structures or models. For instance, the United Kingdom has recently established the Advanced Research & Invention Agency (ARIA), while NATO has established the Defense Innovation Accelerator for the North Atlantic (DIANA), which is directly inspired by DARPA.

DARPA's role in the formation of the Silicon Valley as an innovation hub highlights its influence on regional economic development. By linking academia, industry, and government — the triple helix model — it facilitated the emergence of a vibrant entrepreneurial ecosystem that became a magnet for talent and investment from around the world. Silicon Valley has since become synonymous with technological innovation and entrepreneurship, and its model has been replicated in various forms across the globe.

In addition to fostering a thriving ecosystem, DARPA's approach has also shaped the evolution of venture capital and financing for innovation. By providing substantial funding for high-risk, high-reward projects, DARPA has demonstrated the viability and potential of this investment model, paving the way for the rise of venture capital and other forms of risk-tolerant financing.

Finally, DARPA's work has underscored the importance of building robust infrastructure to support innovation. From research facilities to innovation networks, DARPA has shown that providing the necessary infrastructure can significantly accelerate the pace of innovation. This lesson is particularly crucial for developing countries seeking to foster their own innovation ecosystems.

In summary, DARPA's influence extends far beyond the technologies it has helped to create. It has redefined the innovation landscape, shaped the evolution of innovation ecosystems, and provided valuable lessons for managing and fostering innovation at a systemic level. These lessons and insights are critical for countries and organizations seeking to drive economic growth and societal progress through innovation.

Postwar Economic Recovery

The Ukrainian economy, prior to the Russian invasion in February 2022, was indeed making significant strides toward becoming more innovation-driven and knowledge-based. This shift was primarily driven by the country's burgeoning startup and IT ecosystems, which were proving to be a powerful engine for economic growth and development.

The success of these sectors can be attributed to a combination of factors. First and foremost, Ukraine has a wealth of talent in the areas of technology and entrepreneurship. The country's educational system, particularly in the fields of math, science, and engineering, has produced a large number of highly skilled professionals. This talent pool has been a major draw for international tech companies, which have set up research and development centers in Ukraine, as well as for local startups. Second, the Ukrainian government, recognizing the potential of the IT and startup sectors, has implemented a range of policies to support their development. These include tax incentives for IT companies, initiatives to improve the business environment for startups, and efforts to attract foreign investment into these sectors.

The results of these efforts are clear. Over a 15-year period, the country has seen the emergence of three decacorns (companies valued at over $10 billion) and five unicorns (companies valued at over $1 billion), not to mention 30 dynamically growing and 1368 early-stage startups all created by local entrepreneurs and engineers. Meanwhile, IT service exporters achieved more than 4% of the national GDP employing over 285 thousand high-paid tech professionals. Thus, altogether, startup and the IT market left traditional oligarchs far behind. These VC and high-tech sectors have not only created wealth and jobs but also helped to diversify the Ukrainian economy, reducing its reliance on traditional industries dominated by oligarchs. The success of the IT and startup sectors has also had a broader impact on Ukrainian society, helping to foster a culture of innovation and entrepreneurship and raising the country's international profile as a tech hub.

Gaining increasingly innovative capital, tacit knowledge, and international business development expertise, Ukrainian startup and IT industries launched capitalization and technological convergence spirals that promised to foster further economic advancement. However, the leap from the post Soviet depleted economy to an innovation-driven democratic country has been disrupted, raising the necessity of a future postwar recovery vision.

Being a foundation of outstanding economic development and growth, the world of innovations is swirling in uncertainty and risks on the one hand and exponential opportunities on the other. This magnet creative and entrepreneurial minds to fulfil their vision, hidden from others, and to take on more responsibility by starting risky ventures that, at the end of the day, contribute to common well-being. However, the momentum of their development and implementation heavily depends on early-stage financing when uncertainty and risks are at the highest level.

Whereas remaining incapable of understanding the nature of startup risks and clearly estimating their value because of a lack of proper methodologies and tools, investors tend to avoid dealing with 'black box' investments in favor of traditional low-risk alternatives. It puts them in a vicious circle as, recalling interdependence of the innovativeness level and risks, investors or investment decision makers, thus skipping opportunities with exponential growth potential. This is relevant to private, business and state investors. As a result, it bottlenecks the systemic building of an innovation ecosystem, stifling startup ideas even in the inception stage.

However, innovation is no more a filo stone than a predictable and manageable substance applying the hypothesis testing method (HTM) to evaluate and manage the risks of startups in a quite simple and fast manner. Therefore, we consider a broad application of the hypothesis testing framework and method as a booster for the systemic development of innovation ecosystems and startups, especially important for postwar economic recovery, which is a subject for further research.

Extrapolating from the experiences of DARPA and Israel, the key to economic recovery and skyrocketing lies in nurturing a robust innovation ecosystem. The primary takeaway from these models is the significance of creating an environment that fosters collaboration between government, academia, and industry. This "triple helix" model is characterized by the ability to drive technological innovation, which in turn stimulates economic growth and prosperity.

In the case of DARPA, we have seen how a government agency can effectively stimulate innovation by prioritizing high-risk, high-reward projects. DARPA's role extends beyond mere funding; they also act as orchestrators, fostering collaboration between different stakeholders and ensuring projects align with national goals. They facilitate a process where technological challenges are shared openly with academia and industry, who then compete and cooperate to deliver innovative solutions. This has led to breakthroughs such as the Internet, GPS systems, Artificial Intelligence, and many others, revolutionizing entire industries and contributing significantly to economic growth.

Israel, on the other hand, offers an example of how a country can leverage its unique circumstances to foster innovation. Despite its small size and lack of natural resources, Israel has transformed itself into a global tech powerhouse thanks to its focus on human capital and innovation. The country's compulsory military service has played an unexpected role in this transformation, providing young people with high-tech training and fostering a problem-solving mindset. Moreover, Israel's government has been proactive in promoting innovation, providing financial incentives for R&D and creating an environment conducive to entrepreneurship.

The postwar recovery of Ukraine's economy will undoubtedly be a complex and challenging process. However, by learning from the experiences of entities such as DARPA and countries such as Israel, Ukraine can position itself not only to recover but also to build a more resilient, innovative, and prosperous economy for the future. Drawing from examples of DARPA and Maf'at, Ukraine could consider the following strategies for its postwar economic recovery:

1. **Strengthen Collaboration:** Similar to DARPA, the Ukrainian government could play a key role in promoting collaboration between academia, industry, and government. This would involve not only funding research but also facilitating partnerships and knowledge exchange.

2. **Emphasize High-Risk, High-Reward Projects:** Encourage the pursuit of ambitious, potentially transformative projects. While these projects come with a high risk of failure, they also offer the potential for significant economic and societal rewards.

3. **Promote an Innovation Culture:** Strengthen an environment that encourages entrepreneurship and risk-taking. This could involve providing financial incentives for startups, improving legal protections for businesses, and investing in education and training in STEM fields.

4. **Leverage Unique Strengths:** Similar to Israel, Ukraine should look to its unique strengths as a source of competitive advantage. This could involve capitalizing on its existing pool of tech talent or leveraging its strategic location between Europe and Asia to attract foreign investment.

5. **Broad Application of Hypothesis Testing Method:** Applying the Hypothesis Testing Method can aid in managing the risks associated with innovative startups. By providing a framework for systematically evaluating assumptions, this approach can help attract investment into the sector, providing much-needed capital for early-stage startups.

6. **Establish Innovation Clusters:** Similar to Silicon Valley, fostering innovation clusters can help concentrate resources, talent, and knowledge in specific geographic locations. By providing shared infrastructure and encouraging collaboration between startups, academia, and established businesses, these clusters can drive innovation and economic growth.

7. **Develop sector-specific strategies:** Identify and prioritize sectors with the highest potential for growth and innovation, such as IT, renewable energy, biotechnology, or advanced manufacturing. By targeting resources and policy initiatives toward these industries, Ukraine can foster more impactful innovation and economic development.

8. **Encourage Corporate Innovation:** Incentivize established companies to collaborate with startups, invest in R&D, and adopt more innovative business models. This could involve tax breaks for corporate R&D or partnerships between large companies and startup incubators or accelerators.

9. **International Cooperation and Partnerships:** Foster international collaboration by participating in joint research projects, establishing partnerships with foreign universities and research institutions, and attracting multinational companies to invest in Ukraine's innovation ecosystem. This can help drive knowledge transfer, access to capital, and global market opportunities.

10. **Strengthen Intellectual Property Rights:** Implement robust intellectual property protections to encourage innovation and provide assurance to investors and entrepreneurs that their ideas and inventions will be safeguarded. This could involve improving patent enforcement, simplifying the patent application process, and offering legal support to startups and inventors.

11. **Develop a Skilled Workforce:** Invest in education and training programs to develop a workforce skilled in STEM fields and entrepreneurship. Initiatives could include specialized courses at universities, vocational training programs, and mentorship opportunities connecting experienced entrepreneurs with aspiring innovators.

12. **Foster a Supportive Regulatory Environment:** Streamline regulations to reduce barriers to entry for startups and encourage experimentation. This could involve easing licensing requirements, simplifying tax codes, and offering regulatory "sandbox" environments where new technologies can be tested without the burden of full regulatory compliance.

By adopting these strategies, Ukraine can further strengthen its innovation ecosystem, attract investment, and create an environment where new ideas and technologies can flourish. In turn, this can help accelerate the country's postwar economic recovery and pave the way for long-term growth and prosperity.

Afterword

The unknown frightens people, and new knowledge generates it. After all, the more we know, the more we realize the complexity of a subject area we understand. Therefore, the implementation and spread of new, more complex techniques face resistance, as plunging into uncertainty provokes anxiety. The stronger this anxiety is when the question concerns decision-making and personal capital, responsibility for the future unknown, career, and confidence in the future.

Human nature is designed in such a way that the protective mechanisms of the psyche contribute to ignoring risks. The more such risks there are in a particular decision, the greater the resistance. However, we are faced with a choice — the convergence of technologies and the speed of changes in the competitive landscape do not leave us with the slightest chance of survival if we are not able to adapt. Adapt consciously.

Remember that without understanding the nature of risks, they can neither be measured nor managed. In the ostrich position, we are much more vulnerable.

References

Adams, R., Bessant, J., Phelps, R. (2006). Innovation management measurement: A review. *International Journal of Management Reviews, 8(1), 21-47.*

Aiken, M., Hage, J. (1971). The organic organization and innovation. *Sociology, 5(1), 63-82.*

Albors, J., Igartua-Lopez, I., Peiro-Signes, A. (2018). Innovation management techniques and tools: Its impact on firm innovation performance. *International Journal of Innovation Management, 22(2), 1-31.*

Altshuler, A., Behn, R. D. (1997). Innovation in American Government: Challenges, Opportunities, and Dilemmas. *Washington, D.C.: Brookings Institution Press.*

Amram, M., Kulatilaka, N. (1998). Real Options: Managing Strategic Investment in an Uncertain World. *Oxford, UK: Oxford University Press.*

Anderloni, F. (2011). Project Valuation Using Real Option Analysis. *University of Padova: Department of Information Engineering, 1-49.*

Andrew, J. P., Sirkin, H. L., Butman, J. (2007). Payback: Reaping the Rewards of Innovation. *Boston, MA: Harvard Business Review Press.*

Antoniolli, P. D., Lima, C., Argoud, T., Batista, C. J. (2015). Lean office applied to ICT project management: autoparts company case study. *IPASJ International Journal of Management (IIJM), 3(6), 9-20.*

Assink, M. (2006). Inhibitors of disruptive innovation capability: a conceptual model. *European Journal of Innovation Management, 9(2), 215-33.*

Bell, M., Pavitt, K. (1995). The Development of Technological Capabilities. In: Trade, Technology and International Competitiveness. *Washington: The World Bank.*

111

Berglund, H., Sandström, C. (2013). Business Model Innovation from an Open Systems Perspective: Structural Challenges and Managerial Solutions. *International Journal of Product Development, 18(3/4), 274-85.*

Berkhout, A. J., Duin, P. A. (2007). New ways of innovation: an application of the cyclic innovation model to the mobile telecom industry. *International Journal of Technology Management, 40(4), 294-309.*

Bertels, H., Koen, P. (2013). Business Model Innovation: Innovations Outside the Core. Chapter Four. The PDMA handbook of new product development (3rd ed.). *Hoboken, New Jersey: John Wiley & Sons, 68-81.*

Betz, F. (1993). Strategic Technology Management. *New York: McGraw-Hill.*

Bibarsov, K., Khokholova, G., Okladnikova, D. (2017). Conceptual Basics and Mechanism of Innovation Project Management. *European Research Studies Journal, 10(2B), 224-35.*

Bierman, H., Smidt, S. (2007). Advanced Capital Budgeting: Refinements in the Economic Analysis of Investment Projects. *New York: Routledge.*

Birkinshaw, J., Hamel, G., Mol, M. J. (2008). Management innovation. *Academy of Management Review, 33(4), 825-45.*

Bowers, J. A., Khorakian, A. (2014). Integrating risk management in the innovation project. *European Journal of Innovation Management 17 (1): 25-40.*

Brandão, L., Dyer, J. S. (2005). Decision Analysis and Real Options: A Discrete Time Approach to Real Option Valuation. *Annals of Operations Research, 135(1), 1-25.*

Buchholz, K. (2021). The world's most innovative countries. *The World Economic Forum, 30 September.* Available at: https://www.weforum.org/agenda/2021/09/worlds-most-innovative-countries-innovation/ (Accessed: 28 November 2022).

Casadesus-Masanell, R., Zhu, F. (2013). Business model innovation and competitive imitation: The case of sponsor-based business models. *Strategic Management Journal, 34(4), 464-82.*

Cassia, L., Plati, A., Vismara, S. (2007). Equity valuation using DCF: A theoretical analysis of the Long-Term hypotheses. *Investment Management and Financial Innovations, 4(1), 91-107.*

Cesário, M., Fernandes, S. (2019). Smart innovation strategy and innovation performance: An empirical application on the Portuguese small and medium-sized firms. *Regional Science Policy & Practice, 11(6), 969-82.*

Cetindamar, D., Phaal, R., Probert, D. (2009). Understanding technology management as a dynamic capability: A framework for technology management activities. *Technovation, 29(4), 237-46.*

Chambers, C. P., Echenique, F. (2018). On Multiple Discount Rates. *Econometrica, 86(4), 1325-46.*

Chappin, M. M. H., Faber, J., Meeus, M. T. H. (2019). Learning patterns in early-stage R&D projects: empirical evidence from the fibre raw material technology project in the Netherlands. *R&D Management 49 (4): 684–95.*

Chesbrough, H. (2010). Business Model Innovation: Opportunities and Barriers. *Long Range Planning, 43(2-3), 354-63.*

Chesbrough, H., Lettl, C., Ritter, T. (2018). Value Creation and Value Capture in Open Innovation. *Journal of Product Innovation Management, 35(6), 930-38.*

Christensen, C. (1997). The Innovator's Dilemma: When New Technologies Cause Great Firms to Fail. *Boston, MA: Harvard Business Review Press.*

Christensen, C., Anthony, S.D., Roth, E.A. (2004). Seeing What's Next: Using Theories of Innovation to Predict Industry Change (1st ed.). *Boston, MA: Harvard Business Review Press.*

Christensen, C., Raynor, M. (2003). The innovator's solution: creating successful growth. *Boston, MA: Harvard Business Review Press.*

Ćirić, D., Lalić, B., Gračanin, D. (2016). Managing Innovation: Are Project Management Methods Enemies or Allies. *International Journal of Industrial Engineering and Management (IJIEM), 7(1), 31-41.*

Cooper, R. G. (2010). The Stage-Gate Idea to Launch System. *Wiley International Encyclopedia of Marketing, 1-9.*

Cooper, R. G. (2011), Winning at new products: Creating value through innovation (4th ed.). *New York: Basic Books.*

Cooper, R. G. (2014). What's next? After Stage-Gate. *Research-Technology Management, 157(1), 20-31.*

Cooper, R. G. (2016). Agile-Stage-Gate hybrids: The next stage for product development. *Research-Technology Management, 159(1), 21-29.*

Cooper, R. G., Sommer, A. F. (2016). The Agile–Stage-Gate Hybrid Model: A Promising New Approach and a New Research Opportunity. *Journal of Product Innovation Management, 33(5), 1-14.*

Correia, C., Flynn, D., Uliana, E., Wormald, M. (2007). Financial management (6th ed.). *Cape Town: Juta.*

Damanpour, F., Aravind, D. (2012). Managerial innovation: Conceptions, processes, and antecedents. *Management and Organization Review, 8(2), 423-54.*

Damanpour, F., Gopalakrishnan, S. (2001). The Dynamics of the Adoption of Product and Process Innovations in Organizations. *Journal of Management Studies, 38(1), 35-65.*

Damodaran, A. (2002). Investment Valuation: Tools & Techniques for Determining Any Asset. *New York: John Wiley & Sons.*

Dankbaar, B. (2003). Innovation management in the knowledge economy. *London: Imperial College Press.*

Davila, T., Epstein, M., Shelton R. (2006). Making Innovation Work: How to Manage It, Measure It, and Profit from It. Philadelphia, Pennsylvania: *Wharton Publishing.*

Deak, C. (2009). Managing Innovation Projects versus Ordinary Project Management. *2nd ISPIM Innovation Symposium: Stimulating Recovery – The Role of Innovation Management. New York, 1-8.*

Dean, J. (1951). Capital Budgeting. *New York: Columbia University Press.*

Dodgson, M., Gann, D. (2010). Innovation: A Very Short Introduction. *Oxford, UK: Oxford University Press.*

Drucker, P. F. (2007). Management Challenges for the 21st Century. *New York: Routledge.*

Drucker, P. F., Christensen, C. M., Govindarajan, V. (2013). HBR's 10 Must Reads on Innovation. *Harvard Business Review.*

Dundon, E. (2002). The Seeds of Innovation: Cultivating the Synergy That Fosters New Ideas. *New York: AMACOM.*

Ettlie, J. E., Elsenbach, J. M. (2006). Modified Stage-Gate® Regimes in New Product Development. *Journal of Product Innovation Management, 24(1), 20-33.*

Ettlie, J. E., Reza, E. M. (1992). Organizational integration and process innovation. *The Academy of Management Journal, 35(4), 795-827.*

Fagerberg, J. (2004). Innovation: A Guide to the Literature. *The Oxford Handbook of Innovation. Oxford: Oxford University Press, 1-22.*

Fagerberg, J., Mowery, D., Nelson, R. (2004). Innovation: A Guide to the Literature. *The Oxford Handbook of Innovation. Oxford: Oxford University Press, 1-26.*

Foster, J. (2010). Productivity, creative destruction and innovation policy: Some implications from the Australian experience. *Innovation: Management, Policy & Practice, 12(3), 355-68.*

Frank, A. G., Ribeiro, J. L. D., Cortimiglia, M. N., Oliveira, L. S. (2016). The effect of innovation activities on innovation outputs in the Brazilian industry: Market-orientation vs. technology-acquisition strategies. *Research Policy 45: 577–92.*

Furr, N., Dyer, J. (2014). The Innovator's Method: Bringing the Lean Start-up into Your Organization. *Boston, MA: Harvard Business Review Press.*

Gans, J. (2017). The disruption dilemma. *Cambridge, MA: The MIT Press.*

Garcia, R., Calantone, R. (2002). A critical look at technological innovation typology and innovativeness terminology: a literature review. *The Journal of Product Innovation Management, 19(2), 110-32.*

Goffin, K., Mitchell, R. (2017). Innovation Management: Effective strategy and implementation. *London, UK: Palgrave Macmillan.*

Hall, J. (2006). Environmental Supply Chain Innovation. Greening the Supply Chain. *London: Springer-Verlag, 233-49.*

Hamel, G. (2006). The why, what and how of management innovation. *Harvard Business Review, 84(2), 72-84.*

Hamel, G., Green, W. (2007). The Future of Management. *Cambridge, MA: Harvard Business School Press.*

Hardy, J. (2020). History of Silicon Valley. *History Cooperative.* Available at: https://historycooperative.org/history-of-silicon-valley/ (Accessed: 22 November 2022).

Hartwig, S., Mathews, S. (2020). Innovation Project Risk Analytics: A Preliminary Finding. *Research-Technology Management 63: 19-23.*

Harvard Business Review. HBR's 10 Must Reads on Innovation (with featured article "The Discipline of Innovation," by Peter F. Drucker). (2013). *Harvard Business Review Press.*

Hassan, U. l., Shaukat, S., Saqib, M., Naz, S. (2013). Effects of innovation types on firm performance: An empirical study on Pakistan's manufacturing sector. *Pakistan Journal of Commerce and Social Sciences, 7(2), 243-62.*

Henderson, R.M., Clark, K.B. (1990). Architectural innovation: The reconfiguration of existing product technologies and the failure of established firms. *Administrative Science Quarterly, 35(1), 9-30.*

Herbert, A. S. (1996). The Sciences of the Artificial (3rd ed.). *Cambridge, MA: The MIT Press.*

Hornstein, H. (2015). The integration of project management and organizational change management is now a necessity. *International Journal of Project Management, 33(2), 291-98.*

Hurst, P. (1982). Ideas into action development and the acceptance of innovations. *International Journal of Educational Development, 1(3), 79-102.*

Ingersoll, J. E. (2006). The Subjective and Objective Evaluation of Incentive Stock Options. *The Journal of Business, 79(2), 453-87.*

IT Ukraine Association (2021). Ukraine IT Report 2021. *Reports.* Available at: https://reports.itukraine.org.ua/en (Accessed: 26 November 2022).

Jalonen, H. (2012). The Uncertainty of Innovation: A Systematic Review of the Literature. *Journal of Management Research, 4(1), 1-53.*

Kaminsky, A. B. (2006). The Modelling of Financial Risks: The Monograph. Kyiv: Kyiv University.

Kanagal, N. B. (2015). Innovation and product innovation in marketing strategy. *Journal of Management and Marketing Research, 18, 1-25.*

Kavanagh, D., Naughton, E. (2009). Innovation & Project Management—Exploring the Links. *PM World Today, 11(4), 1-7.*

Keegan, A. E., Turner, R. (2002). The Management of Innovation in Project-Based Firms. *Long Range Planning, 35(4), 367-88.*

Keller, R. T. (2017). A longitudinal study of the individual characteristics of effective R&D project team leaders. *R&D Management 47 (5): 741–54.*

Kerzner, H. (2019). Innovation Project Management: Methods, Case Studies, and Tools for Managing Innovation Projects. *Hoboken, New Jersey: John Wiley & Sons.*

Khorakian, A. (2011). Developing a Conceptual Framework for Integrating Risk Management in the Innovation Project. *Stirling, UK: University of Stirling.*

Kim, W. C., Mauborgne, R. (2004). Blue ocean strategy. *Harvard Business Review, 82(10), 76-84.*

Kim, Y., Song, K., Lee, J. (1993). Determinants of technological innovation in the small firms of Korea. *R&D Management, 23(3), 215-26.*

Kock, A., Gemünden, H. G. (2020). How entrepreneurial orientation can leverage innovation project portfolio management. *R&D Management: 1-17.*

Kodukula, P., Papudesu, C. (2006). Project Valuation Using Real Options: A Practitioner's Guide. *Florida: J. Ross Publishing.*

Latimore, D. (2002). IBM Institute for Business Value. *NY: IBM Corporation.*

Lessard, D., Miller, R. (2001). Understanding and Managing Risks in Large Engineering Projects. *International Journal of Project Management, 19(8), 437-43.*

Liyanage, S., Poon, P. S. (2002). Technology and innovation management learning in the knowledge economy. *The Journal of Management Development, 22(7), 579-602.*

Loch, C. H., Solt, M. E. and Bailey, E. M. (2007). Diagnosing Unforesee-able Uncertainty in a New Venture. *The Journal of Product Innovation Management 7: 28–46.*

Lutz, F., Lutz, V. (1951). The Theory of Investment of the Firm. *Princeton, NJ: Princeton University Press.*

Marion, T. J., Fixson, S. K. (2021). The Transformation of the Innovation Process: How Digital Tools are Changing Work, Collaboration, and Organizations in New Product Development. *Journal of Product Innovation Management, 38(1), 192-215.*

Mathews, S., Russell, P. (2020). Risk Analytics for Innovation Projects. *Research-Technology Management 63: 58-63.*

Mattar, M., Cheah, C. Y. J. (2006). Valuing Large Engineering Projects under Uncertainty: Private Risk Effects and Real Options. *Construction Management and Economics, 24(8), 847-60.*

McGrath, R. G. (2010). Business Models: A Discovery Driven Approach. *Long Range Planning, 43(2-3), 247-61.*

Melkas, H., Harmaakorpi, V. (2011). Practice-Based Innovation: Insights, Applications and Policy Implications. *Springer.*

Merrill, H. M., Wood, A. J. (1991). Risk and Uncertainty in Power System Planning. *Electrical Power & Energy Systems, 13(2), 81-90.*

Morris, L. (2011). Permanent Innovation, Revised Edition: Proven Strategies and Methods of Successful Innovators. *Phelan, CA: Innovation Academy.*

Mugge, P., Markham, S. K. (2013). An Innovation Management Framework: A Model For Managers Who Want to Grow Their Businesses. Chapter Two. The PDMA handbook of new product development (3rd ed.). *Hoboken, New Jersey: John Wiley & Sons, 35-50.*

Myers, S. C. (1977). Determinants of Corporate Borrowing. *Journal of Financial Economics, 5(2), 147-75.*

Nagji, B., Tuff, G. (2012). Managing your Innovation Portfolio. *Harvard Business Review, May, 5-12.*

National Research Council. (1987). Management of Technology: The Hidden Competitive Advantage. *Washington, DC: The National Academies Press.*

Newman, J. L. (2009). Building a creative high-performance R&D culture. *Research-Technology Management, 52(5), 21-31.*

Nieto, M. (2004). Basic propositions for the study of the technological innovation process in the firm. *European Journal of Innovation Management, 7(4), 314-24.*

Norman, R. (1971). Organizational Innovativeness: Product Variation and Reorientation. *Administrative Science Quarterly, 16(2), 203-15.*

OECD. (2004). The Fourth Community Innovation Survey. *OECD.*

OECD. (2005). Oslo Manual: Guidelines for Collecting and Interpreting Innovation Data (3rd ed.). *Paris, France: OECD Publishing.*

Ohara, S. (2005). A Guidebook of Project & Program Management for Enterprise Innovation. *Project Management Association of Japan (PMAJ).*

Ohlson, J. A. (2003). Positive (Zero) NPV Projects and the Behavior of Residual Earnings. *Journal of Business Finance & Accounting, 30(1), 7-16.*

Que, J., Zhang, X. (2020). The role of foreign and domestic venture capital in innovation: evidence from China. *Accounting & Finance, 60(51), 1077-110.*

Paulsen, N., Maldonado, D., Callan, V. J., and Ayoko, O. (2009). Charismatic leadership, change and innovation in an R&D organization. *Journal of Organizational Change Management 22(5): 511–23.*

Pinto, J., Mantel, S. (1990). The Cause of Project Failure. *IEEE Transactions on Engineering Management 37: 269–76.*

Polder, M., Leeuwen, G. V., Mohnen, P., Raymond, W. (2010). Product, process and organizational innovation: drivers, complementarity, and productivity effects. *SSRN Electronic Journal, 1-44.*

Porter, M. E. (1998). Clusters and New Economics of Competition. *Harvard business review, 76(8), 77-90.*

Project Management Institute. (2017). A Guide to the Project Management Body of Knowledge (PMBOK Guide), 6th ed. *Newtown Square, PA: Project Management Institute.*

Que, J., Zhang, X. (2020). The role of foreign and domestic venture capital in innovation: evidence from China. *Accounting & Finance 60 (51): 1077-110.*

Ramirez, N. (2002). Valuing Flexibility in Infrastructure Developments: The Bogota Water Supply Expansion Plan. *Cambridge, MA: MIT.*

Razak, A.A., White, G.R.T. (2015). The Triple Helix model for innovation: A holistic exploration of barriers and enablers. *International Journal of Business Performance and Supply Chain Modelling, 7(3), 278-291.*

Razeghi, A. (2008). The Riddle: Where Ideas Come From and How to Have Better Ones. *San Francisco, CA: John Wiley & Sons.*

Reguia, C. (2014). Product Innovation and the Competitive Advantage. *European Scientific Journal, 1, 140-57.*

Rogers, E. M. (2003). Diffusion of Innovations (5th ed.). *New York: Free Press.*

Rong, Z., Xiao, S. (2016). Innovation-Related Diversification and Firm Value. *European Financial Management, 23(3), 475-518.*

Rothwell, R. (1994). Towards the Fifth-generation Innovation Process. *International Marketing Review, 11(1), 7-31.*

Sánchez-Fernández, Raquel, M., Ángeles Iniesta-Bonillo and Morris B. Holbrook. (2009). The Conceptualisation and Measurement of Consumer Value in Services. *International Journal of Market Research 51: 93–113.*

Sandström, C., Berglund, H., Magnusson, M. (2014). Symmetric Assumptions in the Theory of Disruptive Innovation: Theoretical and Managerial Implications. *Creativity and Innovation Management, 23(4), 1-28.*

Schilling, M. A. (2012). Strategic Management of Technological Innovation. *New York: McGraw-Hill.*

Schumpeter, J. (1934). The Theory of Economic Development. *Cambridge, MA: Harvard University Press.*

Shestakov, D. (2021). The Hypotheses Testing Method for Evaluation of Startup Projects. *Journal of Economics and Management Sciences, 4(4).*

Shestakov, D. (2018). Understanding Innovation: Process, Project and Product-Centric Views. *The Effective Economy, 12, 1-10.*

Shestakov D. (2018). Strategic Flexibility as a Key to Innovativeness: Theoretical Framework. *Global Conference on Business and Economics (GLOBE), University of South Florida Sarasota-Manatee, USA: Anahei Publishing, 120–131.*

Shestakov, D., Poliarush, O. (2017). Strategy of Innovations Development in Ukraine Part I. Introduction. *Innovations Development Platform.* Available at: https://www.slideshare.net/DmytroShestakov/strategy-of-innovations-development-in-ukraine-part-i-introduction-dmytro-shestakov-oleksiy-poliarush-2017 (Accessed: 26 November 2022).

Shestakov D. (2015). Real Option Approach to Evaluate Strategic Flexibility for Startup Projects. *3rd International Interdisciplinary Business-Economics Advancement Conference (IIBA). University of South Florida Sarasota-Manatee, 360–368.*

Shestakov, D., Poliarush, O. (2019). The degree of innovation: through incremental to radical. *Investments: Practice and Experience, 11, 66-75.*

Sick, G., Gamba, A. (2010). Some Important Issues Involving Real Options. Multinational Finance *Journal, 14(1/2), 73-123.*

Siegemund, C. (2008). Blue Ocean Strategy for small and mid-sized companies in Germany. *Hamburg, Germany: Diplomica Verlag GmbH.*

Skalkos, D. (2012). A novel innovation management process: For applications in fields such as food innovation. *International Journal of Innovation Science, 4(4), 245-58.*

Smith, J., Nau, R. (1995). Valuing Risky Projects: Option Pricing Theory and Decision Analysis. *Management Science, 41(5), 795-816.*

Smit, H. T. J., Trigeorgis, L. (2017). Strategic NPV: Real Options and Strategic Games under Different Information Structures. *Strategic Management Journal 38(13): 2555-78.*

Smit, H. T. J., Trigeorgis, L. (2004). Strategic Investment. Real Options and Games. *Princeton, NJ: Princeton University Press.*

Spanjol, J., Mühlmeier, S., Tomczak, T. (2012). Strategic Orientation and Product Innovation: Exploring a Decompositional Approach. *Journal of Product Innovation Management, 29(6), 967-85.*

Stretton, A. (2016). Some consequences of having two co-existing paradigms of project management. *PM World Journal, 5(6), 1-11.*

Taylor, J. E., Levitt, R. (2007). Innovation alignment and project network dynamics: An integrative model for change. *Project Management Journal, 38(3), 22-35.*

Teece, D. J. (2010). Business Models, Business Strategy and Innovation. *Long Range Planning, 43(2), 172–194.*

Tohidi, H. (2012). Different Stages of Innovation Process. *Procedia Technology, 1, 574-78.*

Triantis, A. (2005). Realizing the Potential of Real Options: Does Theory Meet Practice. *Journal of Applied Corporate Finance, 17(2), 8-16.*

Trimi, S., Berbegal-Mirabent, J. (2012). Business Model Innovation in Entrepreneurship. *International Entrepreneurship and Management Journal, 8(4), 449-65.*

Tsang, E. W. K. (2006). Behavioral assumptions and theory development: The case of transaction cost economics. *Strategic Management Journal, 27(11), 999-1011.*

Turner, J. (1990). What Are Projects and Project Management. *Henley-on-Thames: Henley The Management College.*

Tvyss, B. (1989). Management of Scientific and Technical innovations. *Moscow: Economy.*

UkraineNow (2022). Startup Ecosystem. *UkraineNow.* Available at: https://ukraine.ua/invest-trade/startup-ecosystem-ukraine/ (Accessed: 28 November 2022).

Ulwick, A. (2005). What Customers Want: Using Outcome-Driven Innovation to Create Breakthrough Products and Services. *New York: McGraw-Hill.*

Utterback, J. M., Abernathy, W. J. (1975). A dynamic model of process and product innovation. *Omega, 3(6), 639-56.*

Van Lancker, J., Mondelaers, K., Wauters, E., Van Huylenbroeck, G. (2015). The organizational innovation system: a systemic framework for radical innovation at the organizational level. *Technovation, 52-53, 40-50.*

Van Putten, A., MacMillan, I. (2004). Making Real Options Really Work. *Harvard Business Review, 82(12), 134-41.*

Wang, J. (2017). Structuring innovation funnels for R&D projects under uncertainty. *R&D Management 47(1): 127-40.*

Wang, T. (2005). Real Option in Project and System Design identification of Options and Solution for Path Dependency. *Cambridge, MA: MIT.*

Ward, S., Chapman, C. (2003). Transforming Project Risk Management into Project Uncertainty Management. *Internal Journal of Project Management, 21(2), 97-105.*

Wikipedia (2022). DARPA. *Wikipedia.* Available at: https://en.wikipedia.org/wiki/DARPA (Accessed: 20 November 2022).

Wingate, L. (2014). Project Management for Research and Development: Guiding Innovation for Positive R&D Outcomes. *Auerbach Publications.*

Wonglimpiyarat, J. (2004). The use of strategies in management technological innovation. *European Journal of Innovation Management, 7(3), 229-50.*

Young, K. M. (2020). Long-Term R&D Strategy and Planning. *Research-Technology Management 63: 18-26.*

Zawislak, P. A., Alves, A., Tello-Gamarra, J., Barbieux, D., Reichert, F. M. (2012). Innovation capability: from technology development to transaction capability. *Journal of Technology Management & Innovation, 7(2), 14-27.*

Zhou, K., Li, C. (2012). How knowledge affects radical innovation: Knowledge base, market knowledge acquisition, and internal knowledge sharing. *Strategic Management Journal, 33(9), 1090-102.*

UKRAINIAN VOICES

Collected by Andreas Umland

1   *Mychailo Wynnyckyj*
     Ukraine's Maidan, Russia's War
     A Chronicle and Analysis of the Revolution of Dignity
     With a foreword by Serhii Plokhy
     ISBN 978-3-8382-1327-9

2   *Olexander Hryb*
     Understanding Contemporary Ukrainian and Russian
     Nationalism
     The Post-Soviet Cossack Revival and Ukraine's National Security
     With a foreword by Vitali Vitaliev
     ISBN 978-3-8382-1377-4

3   *Marko Bojcun*
     Towards a Political Economy of Ukraine
     Selected Essays 1990–2015
     With a foreword by John-Paul Himka
     ISBN 978-3-8382-1368-2

4   *Volodymyr Yermolenko (ed.)*
     Ukraine in Histories and Stories
     Essays by Ukrainian Intellectuals
     With a preface by Peter Pomerantsev
     ISBN 978-3-8382-1456-6

5   *Mykola Riabchuk*
     At the Fence of Metternich's Garden
     Essays on Europe, Ukraine, and Europeanization
     ISBN 978-3-8382-1484-9

6   *Marta Dyczok*
     Ukraine Calling
     A Kaleidoscope from Hromadske Radio 2016–2019
     With a foreword by Andriy Kulykov
     ISBN 978-3-8382-1472-6

Book series "Ukrainian Voices"

Sergiy Korsunsky, Kobe Gakuin University, Japan

Nadiia Koval, Kyiv School of Economics, Ukraine

Volodymyr Kravchenko, University of Alberta, Edmonton

Oleksiy Kresin, NAS Koretskiy Institute of State and Law, Kyiv

Anatoliy Kruglashov, Fedkovych National University, Chernivtsi

Andrey Kurkov, PEN Ukraine, Kyiv

Ostap Kushnir, Lazarski University, Warsaw

Taras Kuzio, National University of Kyiv-Mohyla Academy

Serhii Kvit, National University of Kyiv-Mohyla Academy

Yuliya Ladygina, The Pennsylvania State University, USA

Yevhen Mahda, Institute of World Policy, Kyiv

Victoria Malko, California State University, Fresno, USA

Yulia Marushevska, Security and Defense Center (SAND), Kyiv

Myroslav Marynovych, Ukrainian Catholic University, Lviv

Oleksandra Matviichuk, Center for Civil Liberties, Kyiv

Mykhailo Minakov, Kennan Institute, Washington, USA

Anton Moiseienko, The Australian National University, Canberra

Alexander Motyl, Rutgers University-Newark, USA

Vlad Mykhnenko, University of Oxford, United Kingdom

Vitalii Ogiienko, Ukrainian Institute of National Remembrance, Kyiv

Olga Onuch, University of Manchester, United Kingdom

Olesya Ostrovska, Museum "Mystetskyi Arsenal," Kyiv

Anna Osypchuk, National University of Kyiv-Mohyla Academy

Oleksandr Pankieiev, University of Alberta, Edmonton

Oleksiy Panych, Publishing House "Dukh i Litera," Kyiv

Valerii Pekar, Kyiv-Mohyla Business School, Ukraine

Yohanan Petrovsky-Shtern, Northwestern University, Chicago

Serhii Plokhy, Harvard University, Cambridge, USA

Andrii Portnov, Viadrina University, Frankfurt-Oder, Germany

Maryna Rabinovych, Kyiv School of Economics, Ukraine

Valentyna Romanova, Institute of Developing Economies, Tokyo

Natalya Ryabinska, Collegium Civitas, Warsaw, Poland

Darya Tsymbalyk, University of Oxford, United Kingdom

Vsevolod Samokhvalov, University of Liege, Belgium

Orest Semotiuk, Franko National University, Lviv

Viktoriya Sereda, NAS Institute of Ethnology, Lviv

Anton Shekhovtsov, University of Vienna, Austria

Andriy Shevchenko, Media Center Ukraine, Kyiv

Oxana Shevel, Tufts University, Medford, USA

Pavlo Shopin, National Pedagogical Dragomanov University, Kyiv

Karina Shyrokykh, Stockholm University, Sweden

Nadja Simon, freelance interpreter, Cologne, Germany

Olena Snigova, NAS Institute for Economics and Forecasting, Kyiv

Ilona Solohub, Analytical Platform "VoxUkraine," Kyiv

Iryna Solonenko, LibMod - Center for Liberal Modernity, Berlin

Galyna Solovei, National University of Kyiv-Mohyla Academy

Sergiy Stelmakh, NAS Institute of World History, Kyiv

Olena Stiazhkina, NAS Institute of the History of Ukraine, Kyiv

Dmitri Stratievski, Osteuropa Zentrum (OEZB), Berlin

Dmytro Stus, National Taras Shevchenko Museum, Kyiv

Frank Sysyn, University of Toronto, Canada

Olha Tokariuk, Center for European Policy Analysis, Washington

Olena Tregub, Independent Anti-Corruption Commission, Kyiv

Hlib Vyshlinsky, Centre for Economic Strategy, Kyiv

Mychailo Wynnyckyj, National University of Kyiv-Mohyla Academy

Yelyzaveta Yasko, NGO "Yellow Blue Strategy," Kyiv

Serhy Yekelchyk, University of Victoria, Canada

Victor Yushchenko, President of Ukraine 2005-2010, Kyiv

Oleksandr Zaitsev, Ukrainian Catholic University, Lviv

Kateryna Zarembo, National University of Kyiv-Mohyla Academy

Yaroslav Zhalilo, National Institute for Strategic Studies, Kyiv

Sergei Zhuk, Ball State University at Muncie, USA

Alina Zubkovych, Nordic Ukraine Forum, Stockholm

Liudmyla Zubrytska, National University of Kyiv-Mohyla Academy

Friends of the Series